What people are saying about

Emotional Capitalism

Emotional Capitalism critically interrogates the negative impacts of capitalism's growing manipulation of our emotional life and subjectivity through different regimes and discourses. Besides offering a comprehensive analysis of the mechanism of today's emotional capitalism, Peter Lok also asks how "our repressed emotions" which have been "distorted" and "regulated" by "emotional capitalism" can be transformed into "ethical emotions". What kinds of emotional experiences can transform a self-centered subject into an other-centered subject? This book has offered an innovative contribution to the topic of emotional capitalism with theoretical courage and critical insight.

Christian Marazzi, author of *Capital and Affects: The Politics of the Language Economy*

Peter Lok finally gives us the topography of emotion we have been waiting for, from the qualitative to the quantitative and from the passive to the internal and, subsequently, to external action. This heuristic model thus extends itself not only to fields of evolutionary biology, sociology, cultural studies, psychology and politics but also to the more pertinent paradigm of what we could call a *Capitalist Realism* (Fisher) of the twenty-first century.

Charles William Johns, author of *Object Oriented Dialectics: Hegel, Heidegger, Harman*

T0014614

An important contribution to our understanding of the dark and deeply woven threads of emotion which underpin both early and contemporary forms of capitalism and the necessity of protest against it. It was a pleasure to read.

Ron Roberts, author of *Psychology and Capitalism* and *The Off-Modern: Psychology Estranged*

Emotional Capitalism

From Emotional Dictatorship to
Emotional Redemption

Emotional Capitalism

From Emotional Dictatorship to
Emotional Redemption

Peter Wing-Kai Lok
Translated by Mary King Bradley

IFF
BOOKS

Winchester, UK
Washington, USA

JOHN HUNT PUBLISHING

First published by iff Books, 2024
iff Books is an imprint of John Hunt Publishing Ltd., No. 3 East Street, Alresford,
Hampshire SO24 9EE, UK
office@jhpbooks.com
www.johnhuntpublishing.com
www.iff-books.com

For distributor details and how to order please visit the 'Ordering' section on our website.

Text copyright: Peter Wing-Kai Lok 2023

ISBN: 978 1 80341 450 8
978 1 80341 451 5 (ebook)
Library of Congress Control Number: 2022922083

All rights reserved. Except for brief quotations in critical articles or reviews, no part of this
book may be reproduced in any manner without prior written permission from the publishers.

The rights of Peter Wing-Kai Lok as author have been asserted in accordance with the Copyright,
Designs and Patents Act 1988.

A CIP catalogue record for this book is available from the British Library.

Design: Lapiz Digital Services

UK: Printed and bound by CPI Group (UK) Ltd, Croydon, CR0 4YY
Printed in North America by CPI GPS partners

We operate a distinctive and ethical publishing philosophy in
all areas of our business, from our global network of authors to
production and worldwide distribution.

Contents

To Ally

Acknowledgements

My thanks as ever to all those who have contributed to the ideas in this book, either through discussion, shared experience, endorsement, or intellectual endeavour. In particular, I would like to thank Mary King Bradley, Lambert Zuidervaart, Christian Marazzi, Charles William Johns, Ron Roberts, Hui Po Keung, Agnes Shuk-Mei Ku, Lai Chung Hsiung, Albert Cheung, Priscilla Tse, Kwan Yi, and everyone at John Hunt Publishing (especially my personal editorial team at Iff). As ever, I am grateful to my family: Ally, Curtis and Kasper.

For any enquiries you can email me at
peterwklok@yahoo.com.

Preface

Emotional Capitalism: An Analysis of the Libidinal Economy

In recent years, research in the humanities and social sciences has seen the emergence of what is generally called the "affective turn" or "emotional turn". Disciplines within the broader field (cultural studies, gender studies, sociology, anthropology, psychology, political science and philosophy) have all one by one taken the conceptual framework of "feeling", "affect", and "emotion" (I will later give a detailed explanation of these three terms' similarities and differences) as a starting point from which to analyse and critique a variety of social and cultural phenomena. Academics in these fields wish in particular to demonstrate how politics, culture, and economics intersect and mutually influence one another, thereby producing a person's "form of life", identity, and worldview. As Lauren Berlant has pointed out, the emergence of affect theory may be regarded as another developmental stage in the history of ideology, one that calls our attention to understanding, conceptualizing, responding to, and evaluating daily life, with that life being frequently influenced by an unconscious and covert affect that forms our common sense.[1] Because we feel but do not see emotions, they are conveyed to others (a person's body/consciousness) through concrete means such as symbols, intermediaries, and narratives. As a result, the "doing" or production of emotions is required.[2] This aspect of emotion permits the subtle analysis of texts that cultural and media studies enjoy and also opens up a new perspective from which to deal with various texts. It becomes possible to locate not only the symbolic meaning of the texts, but also the different emotions (e.g., pleasure, fear, disgust, etc.) at work within them.

1

There is, of course, the more complicated issue of the terms *affect/affectus*, *emotion*, *mood*, and *feeling*. Although often used interchangeably in the numerous books, papers, and articles about emotion that are being generated today in the humanities and social sciences, three of these terms are related, but not identical. As Brian Massumi points out, *affect* is not personal feeling but pre-personal, while *feeling* relates to the personal and *emotion* is social in comparison.[3] In Western philosophy, it was Spinoza who gave emotion deep thought. In the *Ethics* (the complete Latin title being *Ethica Ordine Geometrico Demonstrata*, or *Ethica* for short), Spinoza points out that people are usually unconsciously affected by a covert, not-easily-articulated intensity of emotion and atmosphere of place, both of which then alter the person's behaviour and consciousness. Affect, which occurs when a person experiences this intensity of emotion, is thus in fact an always in-flux state of mind and body.[4] It acts as a covert drive by which a person can both affect others and be affected. For instance, as a teacher, I am affected by the emotional reactions of the students in my class, which might include laughter, snickering, discontent, headshaking, sleeping, or frowning. While I may not be aware of any emotional intensity at the time, nor have the ability to immediately put my experience into words, I will nonetheless adjust my performance in the classroom. (I might want to tell a joke, for example, to give myself an emotional boost.) Affect is therefore a type of pre-personal consciousness difficult to express in words as well as an emotionally intense, involuntary experience triggered by atmosphere. (It's a bit like when we say that someone has an aura: that person is clearly a single individual, but he or she fills the entire room with an intensity difficult to describe yet definitely felt; then, as a result of this atmosphere, other people in the room unconsciously alter their behaviour.) Affect is therefore a "quantity" of accumulated feeling that combines to a lesser or greater degree with a specific set of surroundings and becomes a moving, collectively shaped, ambiguous, atmospheric force acting on people without their awareness.

If affect is a nonconscious aspect of emotion,[5] then emotion can be described as the display of a feeling such as happiness, disgust, or fear.[6] Others will often share and understand these feelings, so emotion is equated with quality, not the quantity associated with affect. Emotion is to a great extent cognitive, which allows people to understand themselves, others, and the world; it even reflects certain right-wrong, black-white ethical judgements and the worldviews of individuals or groups. (Racism is often the continuous dissemination of one ethnicity's hatred for another.) To further distinguish between emotion and affect, I would refer to the former as "visible": it can be more clearly identified and expressed. The latter is "invisible": it operates prior to consciousness and is barely discernible. Naturally, it is difficult to make a complete distinction between the two while they are in operation, particularly in certain settings. In the workplace, for example, a supervisor who frequently dresses down others and is bad-tempered creates a tense work atmosphere. This atmosphere will over time discipline the employees' workplace behaviour and lead to an unconscious tensing when they step into the office, even if the supervisor is not in that day. This book will use the terms *emotion* and *affect* in a manner similar to the explanation given above. To make the text easier to understand, however, *emotion* will be used more frequently; *affect* will be used only when there is a specific need to do so.

The Emotion of Political Economy

My interest in the emotion of political economy stems from personal observation of today's politics and economy in operation. That both operate through a use of emotion, and in particular an insidious type of affect not easily defined, is increasingly clear. As the scholar Eva Illouz, a specialist in emotional capitalism, points out, emotion is not action; it is instead the internalization of various social and personal interactions. We are thus subject to the control of certain emotions, often without any deep thought or reflection.[7] Consequently, scholars today in the fields of sociology and cultural studies believe that anyone who is currently able to manipulate the popular mood can also to some extent control the direction of social movements and thereby engage in political engineering. As political philosopher Martha C. Nussbaum points out, political philosophy demands the introduction of emotional elements for carrying out in-depth analysis because emotion frequently affects our political judgements. When we dislike a certain ethnic minority, for example, there is actually an underlying value principle at work, yet we seldom give any thought to the emotions that underlie our ethical judgements. Then too, any number of politicians have in fact used emotion to influence the public perception of others (i.e., the disadvantaged and minorities). Underlying everything in today's populist politics, from Trump winning power in the United States to all of Europe rejecting refugees, Muslims, and new immigrants, there is an emotional impetus at work, one which the media, various factions, and governments are not slow in using to manipulate popular emotion. The advantage of emotional manipulation is that it doesn't need to persuade by explaining a large number of social policies, only to make you fear something—in other words, your feelings and body have already taken you in a particular direction before reason has arrived at a full conclusion. An example of this is the recent debate on land supply in Hong Kong. When the government disseminated information about the advantages of land reclamation, it used an appeal to emotion that drew on "fear" for the future (e.g., if we don't reclaim land, our children and grandchildren won't have any place to live) to secure people's support. People received little encouragement to consider the policy's pros and cons.

Western academia already has a number of monographs that address emotional politics and emotional economics. In the 1990s, long before affective and emotional theory became widespread, Lawrence Grossberg, a cultural studies scholar, was using emotional concepts such as "mattering maps" and "affective alliances" to study pop culture fans and social groups (such as rock music fan clubs). He wanted to explain the emotional implications of popular culture by understanding both how these groups used a variety of emotions to organize their lives around that culture and how such emotions affected their patterns of pop culture consumption, manner of use, and identity. (This focus on emotion also quite naturally extended into his more recent criticism of American neoconservatism.)[8] After Grossberg's initial work came Stjepan Meštrović's *Postemotional Society* in 1997; Massumi's *Parables for the Virtual* in 2002; Sara Ahmed's *The Cultural Politics of Emotion* in 2004; *The Affective Turn,* edited by Patricia Ticineto Clough, in 2007; *The Affect Theory Reader,* edited by Melissa Gregg and Gregory J. Seigworth, in 2010; Berlant's *Cruel Optimism* in 2010; and then Ash Amin and Nigel Thrift's *Arts of the Political* and Nussbaum's *Political Emotions: Why Love Matters for Justice* in 2013, to name only a few. All of these used a framework of affective and emotional theory (although their respective theoretical focuses are likely different) to analyse important political, cultural, and economic texts. (Naturally, there has been a continuous stream of similar books, too numerous to mention here.)

As for monographs with a focus on emotion and capitalism, there have been several important works. As early as the 1970s, sociologist Arlie Russell Hochschild proposed the idea of "emotional labor" in her book *The Managed Heart: Commercialization of Human Feeling,* which analysed the phenomenon of alienation in the service industry; in 1990

Michael Hardt used the term *affective labor* to explain how today's capitalism controls human emotion in respect to consumption and production; and in 1996 the Italian scholar Maurizio Lazzarato used the idea of "immaterial labor" to make sense of late capitalism's emotional industries. Lazzarato also wrote *Signs and Machines* in 2014, applying the concept of affect to an exploration of how financial markets make human subjectivity part of the financial system. An analysis that used "affective capitalism" had to wait until Massumi's 2002 *Parables for the Virtual*, in which he considers affect to be both a condition of and infrastructure for late capitalism.[9] Emotional capitalism was the framework for both Illouz's *Cold Intimacies: The Making of Emotional Capitalism*, written in 2007, Martijn Konings's *The Emotional Logic of Capitalism: What Progressives Have Missed* in 2015 and Byung-Chul Han's 2017 book *Psychopolitics: Neoliberalism and New Technologies of Power*. Also in 2017, Iain Ferguson wrote *Politics of the Mind: Marxism and Mental Distress*, which used Marxism to probe the relationship between depression and capitalism. In addition, "affective capitalism" was the theme for the November 2016 issue of the academic journal *Ephemera*. From these examples it becomes clear that scholars now working in the humanities and social sciences have been increasingly designating a characteristic of contemporary capitalism as this long-incubated idea of "emotion/affect".

This book takes up the topic of emotional capitalism with the aim of demonstrating how the capitalism in operation today—which includes managing worker efficiency, merchandising, modelling consumer behaviour, producing economic discourse, etc.—conceals an emotional production and manipulation. Instead of relying solely on computational and stable instruments of rationality, emotion is viewed, in Byung-Chul Han's words, as a "means of production and consumption." By using "high speed" emotion to supersede "slow-moving" rationality, by ensuring capitalism can operate more effectively and at a faster speed, a profit is made more quickly.[10] Economic emotion of this sort is by and large what constitutes the emotional culture that permeates our daily lives—it forms our "emotional style" as Illouz would say,[11] or our "structure of feeling" as Raymond Williams would say. It is, in other words, a set of feelings assembled by life. These feelings, interconnected and charged with tension, unconsciously affect our worldview and the relationship between the individual and the group. As a result of capitalism's excesses, our emotional and mental energies in particular are left overdrawn, weakened, suppressed, or disciplined, and we either burn out or become blind, unable to develop a more effective state of being and ethical capacity.

Thus, this book is not intended as an introduction to emotional capitalism that will explain and promote it, nor is it an analysis of emotional capitalism as a phenomenon. Instead, it aims to give further thought to human emotions as affected by an emotional capitalist society, to consider how we might evolve a sensitivity to social injustice and the suffering of others, and even how we might seek connections with others to form an "emotional community" possessing "ethical emotions" that are "therapeutic" and "redemptive." This book will therefore set out to analyse the following points:

1. How does capitalism produce, discipline, and stimulate our emotions in order to facilitate the operation and consumption of commodity production?
2. How does the operation of capitalism affect human emotions, e.g., how is feeling depressed related to a culture of self-improvement?
3. Can we use autonomous emotional space to counteract capitalism's emotional discipline while subject to it?

4. What sort of "ethics of emotions" do we need in order to form an emotional subject that cares about others and the world? Further, is it possible to promote an emotional politics that responds to the problems contemporary emotional capitalism has posed?

Emotional Capitalism: An Analysis of Libidinal Economics

In order to answer the above questions, I believe it is first necessary to consider a related question concerning emotional and mental energy—how do appropriation, accumulation, production, and consumption assist the effective operation of capitalism in the capitalist production-consumption model? Someone might well respond by asking if Karl Marx addressed emotion. This is a topic academia has discussed at some length. In the 1990s, sociologist Stjepan Meštrović explored emotional capitalism in one of his relatively early works, *Postemotional Society*. In his discussion, Meštrović points out that Marx gave greater weight to the cognitive than to the emotional, and that *The German Ideology* is full of words related to cognition, such as *thinking, conceiving, ideas*, and *forms of consciousness*.[12] Meštrović goes on to say that this fact does not indicate a lack of Marxist discussion regarding emotion, and when Marxists discuss commodity fetishism, alienation, or the irrationality of religion, they are in fact touching on that very issue. But, as Meštrović points out, this class of Marxist ultimately believes that the emotional aspects of human nature must in the end be overcome through heightened consciousness.[13] This is quite different from some later left-wing thinkers such as John Fiske or Antonio Negri, who called for the use of emotion/affect as the impetus for resistance.

One scholar who offers the opposite view, however, is Frank Weyher. While sorting through Marx's *Economic and Philosophic Manuscripts of 1844*, he found that the text's argument places significant emphasis on emotion. Taking a human ontological perspective, Weyher calls attention to Marx's belief that an individual is not only "a laboring being" but also "a sensuous being," and that emotion is the fundamental driving force which guides our acts of free, conscious activity.[14] Although Marx never articulated a comprehensive emotional philosophy, he believed that the body and emotions are necessary for free activity. As he put it, "To say that man is a corporeal, living, real, sensuous, objective being full of natural vigor is to say that he has real, sensuous objects as the objects of his being or of his life, or that he can only express his life in real, sensuous objects."[15] Without emotions (e.g., the five senses), an individual has no consciousness, cannot create an objective world by its application, and has no means of establishing an integral relationship with that world.

Marx also noted that without emotions a person cannot feel the suffering of alienation. By alienation he meant that in a society under capitalist control, people sell their labour power to capitalists, so that it becomes a commodity with an exchange value. As a result, unlike a pre-industrial society, workers no longer own the output of their own labour, nor are they free to do the work they want to do—that is, they cannot freely express their emotions and desires. Marx believed the state of separation which occurs between an individual and that individual's self, tools, work procedures, and outputs from his or her labour is likewise a type of alienation. In other words, our working environment denies us the free use of our intellect and will, and also prevents us from expressing our consciousness and emotions as individuals to the extent that our very natures are violated. Accordingly, Marx stated the following in his *Economic and Philosophic Manuscripts of 1844*:

> Labor is external to the worker, i.e., it does not belong to his essential being... [and] in his work, therefore, he does not

affirm himself but denies himself, does not feel content but unhappy, does not develop freely his physical and mental energy but mortifies his body and ruins his mind. The worker therefore only feels himself outside his work, and in his work feels outside himself. He is at home when he is not working, and when he is working he is not at home.[16]

From clues in the above passage, Weyher inferred that when Marx discussed alienation, he presupposed its emotional element. The suffering of alienation occurs because individuals are sensuous beings who feel hurt and pain. Even though Marx never established a complete theory of emotions, material elements such as emotion and the body were an important aspect of his early theory.

Of course, as a materialist, Marx emphasized class over the psyche when he talked about human nature, thus making any analysis with a focus on emotional or other mental energy far from adequate. Early in the last century, Western theorists contributed several important works inspired by psychoanalysis. These explored how "libido" (Freud's term for an individual's instinctual desires) operates in capitalism, and accordingly carried out a micro-analysis of libidinal characteristics which touched on psychic (i.e., mental) energy. Among these important texts are Herbert Marcuse's *Eros and Civilization*, Gilles Deleuze and Felix Guattari's *Anti-Oedipus: Capitalism and Schizophrenia*, and Jean-François Lyotard's *Libidinal Economy*, all of which attempt to analyse the psychodynamics of capitalism within the psychoanalytical framework of Freud and Jacques Lacan.[17] Here two questions arise. The first is whether psychoanalysis, a field related to human psychology, can be applied to economic analysis. The second is whether "libido" is equivalent to the emotion and affect discussed in this book.

In fact, Freudian psychoanalysis frequently uses the term *libidinal economy*—an economic point of view having to do with mental energy—to describe how an individual's psychic activity (especially sexual desire) operates. Libidinal economy makes use of a mental apparatus that has been preset to transform, stimulate, or delay psychic energy and to keep the energy circulating in it to an absolute minimum. For instance, as certain illnesses seize control over some part of an individual's psychic energy, other activity will be incrementally weakened. (As the energy invested in narcissism increases, for example, there is an inevitable reduction of energy invested elsewhere.)[18] Of course, in the Europe of that time *economy* referred not just to the activities of production and trade but also to the effective allocation of limited resources. Freud used the concept of "libidinal economy" to explain the allocation of finite psychic energy; if libido is neither suppressed nor controlled, individuals will tend to pursue total gratification of sexual desire/pleasure. This is known as the "pleasure principle". That human beings are capable of developing advanced civilization comes down to the fact that they understand how to redirect and even suppress libido: rather than giving their libido permission to head down a single path towards gratification, humans can use their psychic energy to develop a variety of life skills and cultures. This process constitutes a "reality principle". Suppressing libido won't cause it to disappear completely, of course; it will instead hide itself within an individual's consciousness and body, to emerge in various covert and overt forms (such as dreams, jokes, and artistic creation).

Libidinal economy has the additional function of protecting mental health. It can regulate the body, avoiding any excess stimulation from the external world that would lead to various mental and mood disorders. Freud believed that the nonsensical content of dreams results from a mental mechanism that compares, categorizes, and chooses among the various stimuli of daily life. Libidinal economy becomes a gatekeeper for the consciousness, allowing anything important or safe to enter and automatically repressing or sending anything it believes to be unimportant or "threatening" into the subconscious. These items, however, are not in fact completely suppressed. Whatever has been sent to the subconscious waits for an opportunity to make its move, with displacement or distortion permitting it to emerge in dreams (a column or pillar seen in a dream might be a phallus, for example). This process helps to keep an individual's mental state in balance.

1. Marcuse on Eros and Civilization

Freud's concept of libidinal economy inspired a number of later social theorists who extended the economic operating principle of the individual psyche to their study of libido; in doing so, they attempted to determine how the well-oiled operations of today's capitalist society are facilitated by production, displacement, distribution, and repression. In 1955, Herbert Marcuse published *Eros and Civilization*, in which he proposed a critical social theory that combined Marxist theory with Freudian psychoanalysis. In his opening chapter, he points out that Freud's psychology of the individual is essentially a social psychology. Although Freud believed civilization to be the result of the reality principle's suppression of the pleasure principle over an extended period, he nonetheless criticized this long-term subjugation of human instincts because of the suffering and sacrifice it causes. As a result, Marcuse began looking at how capitalism denies and represses libido, an approach which is quite useful for thinking about a political emancipation rooted in libidinal energy.

Marcuse disagreed with Freud that libido is equivalent to sexual desire, asserting that this understanding of it was in fact far too narrow. Instead, it is *eros* that should refer to a quantitative and qualitative increase of sexual desire. To act on eros is to engage not just in sex but in any human activity. Sexual desire is also not necessarily subject to civilization's repressive organization of the instincts, can serve as non-repressive sublimation for the civilization-building ego, and can even be a reactive force. For these reasons, libido can refer to the human pleasure-seeking drive, a biological instinct, or even a kind of "liberated eros" that resists repression to the extent that it sets up a non-repressive system. The key is whether or not eros can be channelled into other public spheres, this being the primary concern of libidinal economy. Hence, the liberation of libido is more than sexual liberation. It is also the effective clearing away of obstacles such that self-sublimation permits libido to sublimate narcissistic desire in favour of civilization building. The result is a happy life capable of satisfying human needs and development:[19] a society oriented towards pleasure, aesthetic creation, and eros.

While Marcuse agrees with Freud that the reality principle can frequently supersede the pleasure principle, he also agrees with Marx that alienation represses libido. Accordingly, he at this point introduces left-wing analysis into his discussion. By using psychoanalysis to bring to vivid life memories and emotions (which may be full of taboos, pleasure, and even trauma) that have been repressed by capitalism and deliberately forgotten by the people, the libidinal energy for social emancipation is redeployed and shifts from the restrictive reality principle back to the pleasure principle.

Similar to Foucault's view, Marcuse also believed that human subjectivity is a social construct constrained by various social codes, and that the reality principle takes a dominant role, thereby overriding individual preference and choice. The capitalists in particular control and repress people's memories and different kinds of phantasy. On the one hand, they use the responsibility of labour, what Marcuse called the "performance principle" (which emphasizes production, competition, profit, utilitarianism, dehumanization/alienation of labour, and rationalism) to repress our libidinal energy for revolution. This repression results in a loss of our remaining freedom and also causes us to forget about the natural resources and power of a liberated life that might be found in our suppressed imagination and memory. On the other hand, capitalism uses consumer culture to alleviate our work pressure. We can, for example, use mindless entertainment culture to give ourselves psychic relief (its use also being a good method for a quick psychic recovery that further emphasizes the alienation of labour). This prevents us from criticizing the problem of alienated labour and guards against the possibility of revolution. As a result, regardless of whether people are working or not working (enjoying leisure time), they actually have no freedom.

Marcuse, however, did not wish to fall into Freud's cultural pessimism, i.e., the thinking that libido is always repressed. On the contrary, he firmly believed in the possibility of liberation. He even more firmly believed in a society without repression (one with no alienation, short work hours, and libidinal energy permitting the true development of human potential), in building non-repressive work and societal relationships, and in the advent of a new erotic reality. Fundamental to all this was Marcuse's assertion that art is of particular importance because its imagination, phantasy, and memory make it the "most visible 'return of the repressed.'" Art is thus able to liberate libidinal energy, bringing people hope and happiness. For Marcuse, genuine art is necessarily a "negation of unfreedom" and also a "Great Refusal" of the reality principle. More than this, it seeks a path to ultimate freedom, a way to no longer live in anxiety. Art's potential liberation is therefore also a displacement of libidinal energy: through either imagination or phantasy, it displaces the repressed state to a state of erotic realization, and so discovers the greater possibility beyond the reality principle—a new, non-repressive reality principle. For Marcuse, the writers Rainer Maria Rilke, André Gide, and

Paul Valéry were artistic heroes because they attempted to realize the human potential for a liberated eros while working within a repressive culture. In addition to these men, he had an especial liking for Friedrich Schiller because he saw in him a blend of emotional experience, rationality, phantasy, and play; there was no need to separate reason and emotion, nor to repress emotion with reason as capitalism did. For Schiller, reason could also be emotion, or the operation of an emotional rationality which allowed a person to break away from reality's control and establish a free life. Marcuse called this "libidinal rationality." Not only does this type of rationality not repress libidinal, emotional, and other energies, it can actually boost their effectiveness, thereby facilitating the new, non-repressive reality principle.

As Marcuse's student Douglas Kellner has pointed out, one of Marcuse's contributions was to establish a libidinal corporeal subject: a flesh and blood being that would both evolve and seek emotional/aesthetic gratification. This concept, which arose from what the modern West saw as the liberation of a purely rational subject that, again, had no need to repress the body or emotions, became a reference for the modern subjects that followed. Marcuse's theory does have flaws, of course. French thinker Bernard Stiegler noted that Marcuse misread Freud's reality and pleasure principles as being in opposition to one another;[20] Freud had in fact pointed out that there would be no pleasure principle without the reality principle, because the pleasure principle is simply a product of desire and not just a drive. In addition to this, Marcuse did not make any strict distinction between pleasure and jouissance[21] and thus failed to establish a more rigorous argument. For Stiegler, who devoted deep thought to libidinal economy, Marcuse nonetheless contributed to our understanding of it. Stiegler not only believed that we should reread Marcuse and the other Frankfurt School thinkers' critiques of capitalism but maintained that without the work of the Frankfurt School, all of his own analyses would have been impossible.[22]

My own opinion is that there is still much to be learned from Marcuse about libidinal economy, especially from his view that libidinal energy is an erotic energy which can lead to the creation of human society, so that as a term it refers to more than just sexual expression. While eros is being suppressed, it is also creative, allowing us to see the breadth and depth of libidinal energy. Can the pursuit of happiness or the assurance of pleasure as the impetus for social reform be libidinal energy's only parameters? Is the liberation of eros in fact human liberation? Can the search for meaning or suffering also bring about social revolution? If the liberation of eros does not occur in tandem with the liberation of the oppressed social classes, or does not become a matter even of disrupting the system, can it still truly be called liberation? In addition to these questions, there is Marcuse's undoubtedly important if brief discussion of the liberation of memory—in today's technological society, however, where digital technology has already stepped in as a substitute for our memory, how do we recover memory's liberating force? What can the true redemptive force of memory be?[23] Moreover, how does capitalism demarcate and bypass our desires on a spatial level? Marcuse does not seem to have discussed these matters in much depth, and so it is perhaps here that we need to further our understanding by looking at the work of three French thinkers: Deleuze, Guattari, and Lyotard.

2. Deleuze and Guattari on the Economics of Desire

In 1972, Gilles Deleuze and Felix Guattari published *Anti-Oedipus*, the first of two volumes comprising *Capitalism and Schizophrenia*, the second being *A Thousand Plateaus*, published in 1980. In *Anti-Oedipus*, they assert that desire is not a "lack" as Lacan suggested; it is instead both revolutionary and productive, a machine that continuously produces energy.

They argue that traditional psychoanalysis sees desire as a purely passive vehicle for social reproduction situated in the context of the "family", not as a social or historical reality that forms an important part of the social substratum. Because the unconscious relationship between an individual's desire and aspects of society, history, economics, and politics is ignored, people fail to recognize that desire is in fact present on a broad scale. As Deleuze and Guattari point out, "It is at work everywhere, functioning smoothly at times, at other times in fits and starts. It breathes, it heats, it eats. It shits and fucks."[24] Their theory thus extends Freud's analysis of desire from the domain of the private family to the whole of society, connecting it in particular to capitalism's modes of production and seeing it in the form of "regimes" able to both produce and regulate desire.

In *Anti-Oedipus*, Deleuze and Guattari state that various social systems control and channel a constant flow of desire, and that capitalism controls or manipulates desire through a process of territorialization/spatialization. In other words, capitalism restricts and regulates the direction of desire's flow or funnels it in a specific direction, as for example when it guides consumer desire to newly developed areas. Conversely, the flow of desire cannot be completely fixed, and as a result, it can cross the boundaries set by social systems and change them via a process of "deterritorialization". The revolutionary desire of Hong Kong's Umbrella Movement in 2016, for instance, transformed Mong Kok's commercialized, consumer desire-filled streets into a space (Mong Kok is a famous shopping area in Hong Kong) for political struggle by a simultaneous process of deterritorialization and reterritorialization. Naturally, powerful capitalism can also simultaneously carry out these two processes: to expand into a new area, capitalists must first transform the place's original meaning, emotion, and flow of desire, then re-encode it (i.e., subject it to various operations that weaken and dissipate the revolutionary energy of desire by assigning it a fixed, symbolic form, such as when the law is used to define which desires are allowed and which are not) as one that allows people to satisfy consumer desire. For example, a desire-producing name is assigned, which allows a consumer space to produce consumer desire, so that the space is re-drawn/constructed/symbolized as one that accommodates only consumer desire. All desire is thus concentrated on consumer products, with all other desires ultimately eliminated (such as the desire to fight for justice). In this way, territorialization creates multiple divisions of space for the production of consumer desire and emotion, and this has led to today's operational norm for emotional capitalism: emotional consumption.

Capitalist economies are also what Guattari would call "subjective" economies, in which various media, economic investment systems, or government policies assemble and embed all independent individuals into a single mechanism. Once people have been incorporated into these "assemblages", they cannot separate at will from the various systems. A person is, for example, unconsciously incorporated into the stock market and becomes an investment-subject integral to investment markets, making state management more convenient. As independent individuals are integrated and transformed into assemblages, each individual becomes what Deleuze describes as a *dividual*, a being with no autonomy, just like numbers, data, or markets.[25] The subjugated dividual often gets "into the game" so to speak due to an implicit, non-representational and asignifying[26] affective/emotional sign. For instance, there is often irrational panic selling in the stock market. When stockholders, subject to a variety of affective/emotional information, blindly give orders to sell, the result is a market crash.

Where Marcuse enthroned the liberation of eros, Deleuze and Guattari raised up the schizo-subject. Strictly speaking, the schizo-subject is not a subject but an assemblage of many different desires that forms a synthetic crystal. It is linked to these desires but is not controlled by restrictive or stifling desire-systems (e.g., family, school, political party). Nor does it remain as any one fully complete aggregation of desires. Instead, it constantly replaces its component desires with a succession of new ones and so continues to produce new subjective states. It may thus be understood as a nomadic subject, or a *body without organs*, which challenges capitalism's stability by escaping the desire-system and remaining in constant flight from capitalism's reality principle. (This concept resembles the "leaderless" social movement that occurred as part of Hong Kong's anti-extradition bill movement in 2019: the protestors' desire to break away from the traditional model for social movements created bonds that transformed the desiring-subjects into a "multitude", their cooperative connections creating the possibility of a new social movement model. They then separated from that multitude to connect with another multitude's desire in a process that endlessly repeats itself.) At a superficial level, the body without organs is a bit like Hong Kong's young people referring to themselves as "rubbish youth" (the equivalent of a NEET— someone who is Not in Education, Employment, or Training) or "buddhists" (i.e., "laid-back" or "zen", as the latter term is sometimes used in the US. An agile consumer culture will of course quickly absorb the shifting signifiers of emotional consumerism.). Both terms convey a sense of escape from social control. But Deleuze and Guattari's nomadic subject differs from a rubbish youth in that the nomadic subject does not wish to evade capitalism by escaping from it, but to carry out revolution.

Even so, for Deleuze and Guattari desire is good only insofar as it can continue to produce; its goodness or badness is not determined by any a priori essentialism. But is it enough to judge desire good or bad based solely on its ability to produce? Fascism's desire was both highly productive and revolutionary, yet that did not make it ethical. Furthermore, how can Deleuze and Guattari, who were inspired by Nietzsche's philosophy of desire, ensure that the desire Nietzsche said is an expression of the will to power does not create a body that subjugates and controls the Other?[27] What kind of subject is the schizo's desiring-subject, exactly? Is it a violent subject? Or an ethically responsible subject? And where does he or she stand in relation to the Other? In addition, apart from desire's continuous growth, what kind of space and what sort of conditions must be in place for humanity to be redeemed? As for the revolution, how will it be carried out and in what direction will it lead (if not towards fascism, at the very least)? As I see it, these questions pinpoint the ways in which Deleuze and Guattari's overall thought falls short in thinking about ethical desire.

3. Lyotard on Marx's Hidden Desire

Jean-François Lyotard, a contemporary of Deleuze and Guattari, proposed a more radical politics of libidinal economy, one that abandoned any critique of Marx's political economy and returned to a Nietzschean politics of desire. Lyotard later rejected the ideas laid out in *Libidinal Economy*, an early work written after the 1968 Paris student movement, calling it an "evil book" arising from his disappointment in left-wing politics. Even so, I consider this book's discussion of libidinal economy to be indispensable.

Lyotard first pointed out that he wanted to Freudianize Marxism by replacing Marx's "political economics" with "libidinal economics." He did not, however, offer a critique of Marx's theoretical standpoint; nor was he attempting to replace the old theory with a new one. He was instead making an earnest attempt to find the libidinal energy concealed in Marx's theory. Lyotard thought we should see Marx's text as a type of madness rather than a theoretical argument. He took the view that Marx was a highly emotional writer and so wished to "stroke his beard as a complex libidinal volume, reawakening his hidden desire and ours along with it."[28] Having read Marx's discussion on the alienation of the worker, for instance, he did not, like Marx, criticize alienation but regarded it quite differently—as a masochistic pleasure for workers:

The English unemployed did not become workers to survive, they—hang on tight and spit on me—*enjoyed* the hysterical, masochistic, whatever exhaustion it was of *hanging on* in the mines, in the foundries, in the factories, in hell, they enjoyed it, enjoyed the mad destruction of their organic body which was indeed imposed upon them.[29]

What Marx saw as suffering, Lyotard saw as a drive for enjoyment and even the pleasure of suffering abuse. Not only did he no longer criticize alienation and exploitation as problematic, but he argued that Marx and left-wing theorists had presupposed alienation based on their conviction that a non-alienated group exists. After having experienced the failure of the 1968 student movement, Lyotard believed the non-alienated person to be little more than a figment of the imagination. Only uncivilized libido remained, a form of naturalism that eliminated ethics and rules and did not allow any possibility of revolution.

Like Deleuze and Guattari, Lyotard viewed society as the flowing of desire and a process of dismantling and restructuring territory. Where they differed is that Lyotard abandoned the traditional intention of social reform and invariably argued the transgressive nature of desire. This ultimately made his libidinal philosophy one of cynicism and evasion. Because *Libidinal Economy* offers essentially no critique of desire, libido, or affect and regards society as uncivilized and saturated in libido, the book as a whole is a failure. As Stiegler said, this is not a good book due to its confusion of ideas, as for example when it equates a drive and a desire without making any distinction between them.[30] I would argue, however, that where it fails is precisely its contribution, because it tells us that an analysis of emotional/libidinal political economy cannot be a discussion that discards ethics and norms with an attitude of "I can do as I like" and "anything goes". This is why the first chapter of this book will first discuss in greater depth various ethics of emotion.

A Pharmacological Critique of Desire and Emotion

So how can this book's proposed analysis of emotion/affect (this introduction began by drawing a distinction between emotion and affect that will not be repeated here) ultimately be integrated with the above works on libidinal economy? In Freud's view, *affect* refers to an emotional state that includes emotions such as suffering and pleasure, and is either the wholesale discharge of emotions or their manifestation as an ordinary mood. All instincts are expressed through affect and mental imagery, while affect (which includes emotion) "is the qualitative expression of the quantity of instinctual energy and of its fluctuations."[31] In his *Studies on Hysteria*, Freud pointed out that hysteria occurs when there is no propositional discharge of affect resulting from a traumatic event—no experience of crying out to express injury, for example—and this turns the wounding experience into emotional detachment or depression, i.e., emotional blockage. Therefore, in Freud's view, emotion is the expression and conversion of instinctual energy; and libido, which exists as a parasite regulating the expression of the various emotions in which it lives, acts as one of these instinctual energies.

Although libido is not the equivalent of affect/emotion, they have a symbiotic or mutually corroborative/performative relationship. For this reason, as today's emotional capitalism increasingly carries out its core operation of regulating the psycho energy of individuals, the need to analyse a variety of methods for emotional production and regulation using the libidinal economic model likewise increases. (In this regard, the work of Freud, Marcuse, Deleuze, Guattari, and Lyotard, as well as the work of Byung-Chul Han and Stiegler, to be discussed later, are of particular use.) This is the only way for us to better understand the characteristics of emotional capitalism, especially the phenomena of emotional production, labour, and consumption. In addition, libidinal economy requires us to understand the wrestling match that takes place between libido's various regulatory and anti-regulatory forces, as when libidinal regulation leads to the "destruction" of consumer desire or the "curative" desire for social reform. Stiegler referred to this type of critique as the "pharmacology of desire." It both eliminates the residual toxicity of desire and brings about its positive release, and as such is a good demonstration of desire's double nature." This type of analysis can help us to reorganize or give us greater access to curative libidinal/emotional energy in the current system and so produce a greater number of new economic, cultural, and political systems which differ from the mainstream systems.

It is not my intention to make a sweeping rejection of emotional capitalism, despite its many problems. Rather, we must always seek out any opening for carrying out reform, expanding the possibilities for a society saturated in libidinal/ emotional energy, even if that opening is only a small one. Desire is not necessarily what Stiegler called destructive "deindividuation." There can also be "transindividualizing" desire that promotes life,[33] desire that leaks out of cracks in the system to constantly make connections with numerous Others, systems, spaces, and technologies of affirmative desire. Ultimately, this type of transindividualizing desire can become a reassemblage of space for already existing emotional capital, or to use Deleuze's terms, it can carry out "territorialization" and "deterritorialization" of capitalism's spaces of desire.

In the first chapter of this book, the theories of Byung-Chul Han will be used to show how emotional capitalism controls, manages, and suppresses the emotions and spirit to meet the operational needs of the libidinal economy. The ultimate cost of this, however, is the creation of individuals concerned only with their own self-interest and achievement. In endlessly seeking to climb the career ladder, these individuals so exhaust themselves physically and mentally that they become indifferent to objects, society, and others around them, and (perhaps without much mental energy left to care) gradually become detached, depressed, and powerless subjects.

In subsequent chapters, I apply the assorted thinking of Bernard Stiegler, Emmanuel Levinas, and Judith Butler, philosophers who discuss the transformation of detached emotions and show how the experiences of aesthetic perception, suffering, and grief change a disaffected, detached subject into an affective, ethical subject (one who can feel moved by the situation of the other). This phenomenon has occurred in several Hong Kong social movements, such as the vigil commemorating the Tiananmen Square massacre on June 4, the Umbrella Movement, and the anti-extradition movement. During all of these, it was common to see subjects actively mourning and silently remembering the suffering other, activities that have transformative ethical power.

I also wish to point out, however, that to analyse only the manner in which emotional capitalism operates is insufficient for confronting its formidable power. Instead, we must also examine its double nature (or what Stiegler calls *pharmaka*—the double nature of medicine as both poison and cure). That is, we must examine whether emotional capitalism can negate life's negativity while also nurturing positivity. At the crux of this discussion are the ways that human emotion and psychic energy are transformed, turned into ethical emotions capable of driving social reform. Ultimately, I hope to enable the transformation of individuals from cold and unemotional subjects to subjects who are emotionally responsible.

Chapter 1

From the Achievement-Subject to the Burnout-Subject: Byung-Chul Han on Emotional Capitalism as Emotional Dictatorship

The body no longer represents a central force of production, as it formerly did in biopolitical, disciplinary society. Now, productivity is not to be enhanced by overcoming physical resistance so much as by optimizing psychic or mental processes. Physical discipline has given way to mental optimization

—Byung-Chul Han

The traditional understanding of capitalism presumes it operates according to an underlying set of rational mechanisms. Working style, employee management techniques, capital investment calculation, commodity sales strategies, consumer behaviour modelling, the production of economic discourse: every aspect is highly controlled through computations and planning. In sociology, the Fordist economic model refers to the automobile production model created by the industrialist Henry Ford. This model, which gave rise to modern methods of industrial production, includes the adoption of streamlined work processes; production lines with a strict division of labour; a highly stratified system of management; a system of higher wages tied to productivity and profit; standardization of mass-produced goods; and a single mass market. To complement this very rational method of production, the high degree of rationality and standardization present in industrial society has been extended to the control of workers' bodies, emotions, and spirits. The workers themselves are likewise required to exercise a high degree of physical control; if they do not, they will be unable to handle the exacting demands of the labour. Watch Charlie Chaplin's *Modern Times*, and it's clear that the body of the worker must be completely in tune with the operations of the machine to achieve an *integration of man and machine*. Workers who lack strong bodies and focused minds cannot meet the needs of businesses.

The German sociologist Max Weber may have been the first to realize that capitalism benefits from the psychoemotional control of workers. In his book *The Protestant Ethic and the Spirit of Capitalism*, Weber notes that the Protestant ethic (also known as Calvinism) is a form of worldly asceticism. As such, it encourages the faithful to control their appetites and emphasizes integrity, duty for duty's sake rather than personal happiness, building a rational body, and seeing hard work and earning a wage as a calling that serves God. This social ethos derived from Protestant ethics is highly compatible with capitalism. Weber gives the example of devout German female workers, these women demonstrating a greater ability to throw themselves into learning new and more efficient work methods than their nonreligious counterparts; he points out that they could do so because of their conviction that work is a religious calling. In today's post-Fordist capitalist society, however, a greater focus on service industries rather than those involving labour has led to more emphasis on managing and caring for the libidinal economy of our personal mental states. We can see that capitalism's control over people's emotional and psychic energy will continue to gain ground and become increasingly complex, so that Foucault's *biopower*[34] may no longer even apply. This is because today we are most likely being controlled not just by biopower, which controls our bodies, but also by *psychopower*, which manages or controls our various mental states. But how exactly does this psychopower produce/connect to each individual emotional labour subject? And what impact does this emotionalization of the production process have on our mental lives? Answers to these questions will be discussed and further analysed by looking at the work of Byung-Chul Han.

The Production and Consumption of Emotional Capitalism

As the Korean-born German philosopher Byung-Chul Han states in his book *Psychopolitics*, the first question to be answered when talking about emotional capitalism is this: Why, having reached its current state of development, does capitalist society require us to experience such a "boom" of feelings? This is a question a number of scholars researching emotional capitalism today have neglected. Eva Illouz's *Cold Intimacies: The Making of Emotional Capitalism*, for example, receives Han's criticism for failing to address it. According to Han, when a neoliberal capitalist society promotes nonmaterial production (e.g., the service industries) so that it can accelerate production and earn profits more quickly, it no longer relies solely on the calculable stability of *instrumental reason*, but increasingly regards emotion as *the means of production and consumption*.[35] In fact, today's workplaces outwardly emphasize personal freedom and emotional growth, such as developing positive thinking or cultivating a high EQ (emotional intelligence), and in contrast to the traditional approach of oppressive discipline, this *emotionalization of the productive process* can increase employee productivity and improve work performance. Furthermore, this trend has demonstrated the superiority of high-speed emotion over slow rationality and thus ensured the effective operation of capitalism.[36] Rationality cannot achieve a continuous increase in production efficiency because it is neither fast enough nor flexible enough. (For example, endless meetings or creating more bureaucracy to handle problems will simply be more time-consuming.) To create a feeling of compulsion or constraint, on the other hand, is easy. (Say, for instance, that you will lose

27

additional income or even be fired if your turnover or orders for the month don't hit a certain amount.) As Han puts it:

> Rationality is defined by objectivity, generality and steadiness. As such, it stands opposed to emotionality, which is subjective, situative and volatile. Emotions arise, above all, when circumstances change—and perception shifts. Rationality entails duration, consistency and regularity. It prefers stable conditions. The neoliberal economy, increasingly dismantling continuity and progressively integrating instability in order to enhance productivity, is pushing the emotionalization of the productive process forward. Accelerated communication also promotes its emotionalization. Rationality is *slower* than emotionality; it *has no speed*, as it were. Thus, the pressure of acceleration now is leading to a *dictatorship of emotion*.[37]

In the context of globalization, neoliberal capitalism is indeed always full of uncertainties and risks, and because of this, companies require employees (especially management) to be able to deal with that risk. For this reason, the greater an employee's control over their own and others' emotions in the workplace, the more successful they are. This is because emotional control can help to accelerate commodity production more effectively and flexibly as well as resolve any technical difficulties. Emotional capital may therefore be more important than cultural capital when it comes to emotional capitalism. To perform well and develop as we should in the workplace, we do need some cultural capital—such as academic qualifications, family background, and even some appreciation of culture and the arts—but in emotional capitalism, the primary emphasis is on managing the body and emotions. (This is not necessarily constraint since a subject requires both restraint and release; rather than aiming for the comprehensive rational constraint of

The Protestant Ethic and the Spirit of Capitalism, a person should work hard, play hard.) In the workplace, good emotional management skills can become a career-boosting advantage and a type of capital.

In other words, how we quantify the amount of emotional capital an individual possesses is extremely important, in that those with lots of emotional capital will also have *emotional confidence*. In her book *Emotional Confidence*, emotional management expert Gael Lindenfield asserts that building emotional confidence is vital because to do so is tied to survival in the workplace. Those with poor emotional confidence may not have the courage to accept a new job, for example, just as frequent angry outbursts can cause trouble at work. Conversely, good emotional confidence can assist in effective communication with colleagues, can save money that would otherwise be spent on antidepressants or sleeping pills, and can help get things done more efficiently; it can also facilitate the achievement of personal work targets by allowing tasks to be successfully completed. Byung-Chul Han has noted that as capital increasingly becomes *immaterial*, people are recognizing that emotions can be a flexible form of productive capital, and that this phenomenon may make class divisions less important. (I don't fully agree with his point here; see my later discussion of emotional labour.) Class exploitation (capitalists exploiting workers) has now become self-exploitation, as in the case of the worker who must maintain a stable mood at all times to carry out his or her work.[38]

The books on emotional management currently on the market stretch practically to the horizon, all of them loudly proclaiming exclusive, custom-tailored emotional equations. Such books have helped us to survive economic difficulties as well as to develop several successful emotional equations for enhancing emotional capital. In his book *Emotional Equations: Simple Truths for Creating Happiness + Success*, Chip Conley, CEO of the renowned Joie de Vivre Hospitality, talks about the suicide of a good friend. The friend was an insurance broker during the 2008 financial turmoil, who took that final step because he was unable to cope emotionally with the impact of the economic storm. This incident prompted Conley to design a series of equations for senior executives. Those who follow his guidelines for managing their emotions are not only able to handle adversity but can also improve their market competitiveness. As Conley says in his book, the most successful business leaders are emotional experts who know "how to use Emotional Equations to create insight and perspective as well as happiness and success."[39] Conley does not reject emotion; he advocates physical and mental health through emotional release. Even so, he does not think this means our emotions control us. Releasing emotions is part of managing them, especially in the workplace, where stress can easily build up. Without that release, our negative emotions are more likely to affect us, and so we must manage emotions just like a supervisor manages money. The better able we are to manage them, the more likely they will increase our emotional capital and work to our benefit. This is why Han observes that supervisors today no longer rely on the principles of rational action and are instead more like motivational coaches.[40] The widely used techniques of rational management are gradually being replaced by those of emotional management.

Han also points out that consumerism is increasingly using emotion to stimulate our wants and needs. The emotional design of products has shaped our consumption patterns—we no longer consume the product itself but rather emotion, and the libidinal economy has given us more outlets for doing so. We engage in consumer activities not only to vent dissatisfaction with life caused by our alienation at work, but also to *sublimate* our negative emotions into more refined, stress-relieving ones. For example, if you visit a high-end restaurant, you no longer want just to satisfy your hunger (*use value*), but also demand that the restaurant's brand act as a status symbol (*sign value*), and that the waiter and dining environment make you happy or even deliver a romantic atmosphere (*emotional value*).

As it happens, Han's discussion of emotional consumption complements the emotional elements appearing in explanations of consumption that Marx and postmodernist theory have given us. During the 1980s, the French thinker Jean Baudrillard proposed that commodities in a consumer society have not just what Marx called *use value* but by necessity also have a *sign value* that can provide consumers with various cultural meanings.[41] Consumers will therefore rely not just on rationality (price, product quality) when considering a product, but will also determine whether or not to consume a product based on the meaning it creates. For example, when we decide to buy a pair of sneakers, in addition to considering their utility (the materials, function, etc.), we give even greater value to how fashionable we perceive them to be as a result of advertising. This explanation begins with the sign value of commodities and points out how consumer culture makes use of an enormous *system of objects* comprising advertisements, magazines, and cultural discourses—a series of symbols form a system that establishes the social and cultural significance of products and encourages consumption. But Illouz, another scholar who studies emotional consumption, has pointed out that this understanding is still inadequate because it ignores that today's commodities aren't limited merely to Marx's use value or Baudrillard's sign value, but also have an *emotional value*:

In *Das Kapital*, Marx defined a commodity as a real item whose value is determined by the amount of time needed to produce it. Then came Baudrillard. He dematerialized the commodity, and it became a set of signs. But emotional commodities are neither the former nor the latter.[42]

31

Han considers the advantage of emotional consumption, like that of emotional capitalism, to be a faster and more effective opening up of an "unbounded" consumer space.[43] Emotional consumption can make emotions and feelings the focus of everyday life, thus giving it the same appeal as a game. In fact, the stimulus of emotion helps to create boundless consumer imagination and desire that ensure a faster rate of return. An emotional capitalist society can continue to expand, relying on the constant transformation of libido into consumer desire. Emotional consumption doesn't allow consumer attachment to specific products, however, as this would stop people from consuming new products and curb profit growth. For this reason, products or products of the same type cannot give people just one feeling that lasts forever; they must continue to produce the sense that they are new and exciting to accelerate the rate of personal consumption. Nor can products create a sense of attachment that makes people unwilling to move on from them, as this would hinder the development of new markets.[44]

Globalization has turned global market integration in the neoliberal economy into an iron law. Because of this, products generate emotions not just to get customers to consume, but also to accelerate the rate at which consumers abandon products. As Stiegler says, products are *temporal objects*. That is, they are not intended to last indefinitely. Instead, they are deliberately designed to have a short life so that consumers will forget them as quickly as possible and consume more products out of their desire for the new. This is what Georges Bataille called *productive expenditure*, an economic system that operates not by accumulating energy but by depleting it, so that a loss of wealth or energy must occur before it can become an endlessly growing, driving force for human society.

From this we can see that emotional consumption does not actually improve our mental state, nor does it bring us the liberation of happiness and freedom. Consumption that is both unfree and compulsive—just as work is unfree—leads to excessive consumption. The problem is not our enjoyment of life, but that in a libidinal economy, work and enjoying life (consuming) are coordinated or even *collaborative* activities intended to control people's mental states so that they will adapt to and support the operation of capitalism. As Han wrote in another of his books, *In the Swarm: Digital Prospects*:

> The neoliberal imperative to perform transforms time into working hours [*Arbeitszeit*]. It totalizes a belabored temporality. Breaks represent only a phase of the working day. Today, we know time only as time for working. And so this temporality follows us not only on vacation but even when we sleep. ... Even relaxation amounts to a mode of labor: it occurs to regenerate working power. Recreation is not the other of work but its product. So-called deceleration cannot generate any other time, either. It is also a consequence, a reflex, of the accelerating working day. It only slows down time for work—instead of changing it into another kind of temporality.[45]

In other words, we should engage in neither work nor consumption since we cannot freely enjoy life until we completely withdraw from the system of capital production. Here we can see that an emotional capitalist society needs our emotions to work in conjunction with/conform to the operations of capitalism, and that this requires two specific methods of psychic manipulation. The first is the mood-controlling *ascetic* style of manipulation, which ensures that work or rest is efficiently and fully carried out in such a way that the worker can continue to work (rest is also a product of work). The second is the *orgiastic* style, which urges people to indulge in endless emotional consumption. Both methods are in fact what Marx called *alienation*, that is, a double alienation of both emotional labour and emotional consumption. Because capitalists control all places of work, leisure, or consumption in a capitalist society, workers never have time that falls into the non-alienated category. Work time belongs to the capitalists, and so does leisure time, even when a person is not at work.

Achievement- and Burnout-Subjects in Emotional Capitalism

Han is concerned not just with how emotional capitalism operates but with the kinds of subjects it produces. In another of his books, *The Burnout Society*, he looks at the ways that contemporary capitalism produces a succession of *achievement-subjects*. While Han doesn't doubt that capitalism disciplines our bodies to bring them into line and suit them to the operations of capitalism, it doesn't necessarily do so through constraint or unfree methods. Instead, it makes greater use of encouragement and positive, affirming methods that boost our psychic energy. He asserts that today's capitalist society is in fact an *achievement society*—one that assigns value to work performance and encourages constant improvement and learning so that an individual can become someone who *meets expectations*. Today's university professors, for instance, are often subjected to evaluations by the university, their students, or some external groups, with their work capabilities endlessly quantified and turned into data sets that judge quality. Underlying all of this quantification is the need to satisfy the achievement society's demand for numbers. If the professor publishes too few papers or submits too few articles to academic journals, a judgement of *does not meet expectations* could affect his or her prospects.

Capitalist society today has no need to keep frustrating our efforts. Instead, it encourages us keep moving up by studying, striving to achieve, and making ourselves into an achievement-subject. The enticements offered by this operational mechanism that pushes people to actively achieve and to say "okay" more often than "no" is what Han calls *smart power*.[46] To borrow terminology from libidinal economics, this *smart power* is the constant stimulation or *inducement* of *psychopower* that channels people's desire into the pursuit of self-expression. Ultimately, the tough, go-getter personality that smart power produces is the same libido-guided narcissistic-obsessional that Freud discusses.[47] Han also notes the maxims of the achievement-subject:

> Its maxims are not obedience, law, and the fulfillment of obligation, but rather freedom, pleasure, and inclination. Above all, it expects the profits of enjoyment from work It works for pleasure and does not act at the behest of the Other. Instead, it hearkens mainly to *itself*. After all, it must be a self-starting entrepreneur [*Unternehmer seiner selbst*]. In this way, it rids itself of the negativity of the "commanding [*gebietender*] Other."[48]

This is an invisible oppression that internalizes others' demands as our own to such an extent that we engage in unconscious self-oppression. Worst of all is that people will experience burnout whether they meet expectations or not, and may even suffer from depression or emotional disorders because they are unable to meet the demands they have placed on themselves.

This achievement-oriented capitalist culture shows up not just in the workplace, but in groups of very young children and students, as well. In fact, the current Hong Kong school system has essentially brought the logic of workplace evaluations into schools. Parents (particularly in middle-class families) arrange interest classes for pre-schoolers. Children take classes for admissions interviews before entering primary school. Secondary school students attend a whole range of homework tutorial courses as well as juggling cram school classes for public examinations. All of this additional practice is to ensure that students can meet the expected standards, but it's also the cause of kids burning out. Most primary and elementary schools in Hong Kong have full-day class schedules, so it's already 5:00 p.m. by the time kids return home. But they have little time to relax even then because there is still homework and reviewing to do. It's frequently 11:00 p.m. before they can take a break, which might mean they have it harder than the adults. And so, the burnout lifestyle doesn't necessarily start when we enter the workforce, as Han says. It has already begun during our school years. We are frequently exhausted, but our tiredness is itself an indication that we have failed to meet the expectations of our achievement society. Conversely, it might also mean that we have already done such a good job of achieving that we must maintain our current level of achievement or even redouble our efforts to achieve even more. We can take any number of successful people as an example: they are often so tired that they will spend the whole day telling anyone and everyone that they plan to retire at age 50; but the only result of this wish is the desire to make money so that they can do so, and they wear themselves out in the process.

Han has also observed that the interpersonal relationships of achievement-subjects are not necessarily positive. When you view those around you as rivals, have no close friends, and see an imagined enemy even in yourself, the result is an unhappier and more depressed person who is even more likely to develop a narcissistic personality. In his book *In the Swarm*, Han takes his analysis a step further, writing that the subject's spirit is never awakened because he/she has no *other* to provide a spiritual shock. It doesn't matter if that shock is sometimes negative:

The *negativity of the other* is what keeps it alive. Whoever relates only to him- or herself, or remains stuck where she or he is, lacks spirit. Spirit is marked by the capacity to "endure infinite *pain*, the negation of its individual immediacy." The positive, which strips the other of all negativity, degrades into "dead nature."[49]

This view derives from Hegel[50] as well as Levinas,[51] both of whom think that the negative energies of the other (such as pain) form the subject's primary source of experience. Naturally, the many instances of positive experience (such as love) that the other gives the subject should not be overlooked; Han is simply pointing out that the self-sufficient subject often has only a one-dimensional relationship with the self and, unable to experience the struggle of love and hate with an external other, is ultimately unable to form any experience at all.

Han has expanded the Italian philosopher Giorgio Agamben's concept of *homo sacer*, or the *sacred/accursed man*,[52] by drawing a comparison between the *homo sacer* of medieval Roman times and its contemporary form. In medieval times, people falling into this category could be killed, often thanks to a *state of exception*, by a sovereign that viewed them as expendable, as worthless *bare life*. In today's achievement society, however, *homo sacer* has become the *achievement-subject*, "killed" by work in a *totalized state of normality* or *state of positivity*. "Death" occurs because the achievement-subject is often presented with an *idealized self* that results in self-blame for being a perpetual loser never able to meet expectations. This puts the self into a state of constant tension that ultimately forces it into the self-destructive dilemma of *auto-compulsion*. This is essentially the *violence of positivity* in what ought to be negative experiences of burnout and depression:

The capitalist system is switching from allo-exploitation to auto-exploitation in order to accelerate. On the basis of the paradoxical freedom it holds, the achievement-subject is simultaneously perpetrator and victim, master and slave.

Freedom and violence now coincide. The achievement-subject that understands itself as its own master, as *homo liber*, turns out to be *homo sacer*. ... By this paradoxical logic, sovereign and *homo sacer* still generate each other in achievement society.[53]

To put it bluntly, capitalism tells us to think of life as a special project, yet we find ourselves caught in a negative loop, unable to create a good-looking curriculum vitae that meets society's expectations, which in turn makes it difficult to find satisfying work. When this situation is coupled with the inevitable daily grind of *bullshit jobs*,[54] the disappointment we feel in ourselves can easily lead to depression.

Yet I would also like to point out that the positive thinking present in most of today's popular psychology has also played a role in achievement-society discourse. This is *chicken soup for the soul* that tells you to get to it with an *optimistic* and *positive* attitude and rejects the *positivity* of *venting*. It tells people to just stop being depressed and change the negative perspective underlying that mood. On the surface, discourses like these appear to be healthy, but they are in fact constantly intensifying our inner self-oppression, giving us no time to examine the psychological and emotional problems that an achievement society creates. For instance, the modern capitalist society, like Hong Kong, appreciates only those who are positive and positivity-oriented, whereas those who experience depression and comparatively negative emotions, or who tend to be *particularistic*, have greater difficulty taking part in the current social system.

In her book *Bright-Sided: How Positive Thinking Is Undermining America*, Barbara Ehrenreich, a cellular biologist who has dedicated herself to social activism, points out that when today's economists measure a country or region's economic achievement, they look not just at the gross national product but also measure people's happiness.[55] In fact, capitalist society has always used the upbeat happiness of positive thinking as a method of overcoming economic difficulties. Ehrenreich points out that when employment in the United States began to decline in the 1970s and 1980s, corporations were laying off large numbers of employees and cutting benefits to deal with the economic crisis. To control their employees' feelings of hopelessness and anxiety, corporations were constantly encouraging them to "think positive." They prevented and controlled workers' pessimism, and even told them to do their work with a sense of gratitude. In the United States of the twenty-first century, the activities intended to motivate employees aren't just superfluous programs; they have penetrated the very core of American companies and prevent the panic caused by economic downturn – panic which in turn impacts productivity. Meanwhile, numerous treatises on positive thinking (such as *In Search Of Excellence* and *Who Moved My Cheese*), coaching, and group activities have appeared, all of which seek to help employees face life's difficulties with a positive, optimistic attitude and straighten out negative thinkers. As a result, *positive thinking* has been commercialized while also becoming doctrine. It suppresses the unique personalities of individuals and ignores real social problems, invariably telling people to immerse themselves in blind optimism.

Ehrenreich argues that positive thinking's happy outlook isn't necessarily the best method for dealing with life's pain. Sometimes engaging in self-deception to maintain a positive mood can cause a more serious emotional problem:

[Positive thinking] requires deliberate self-deception, including a constant effort to repress or block out unpleasant possibilities and "negative" thoughts.[56]

The biggest problem here is that we often see ourselves as the enemy—we drive a wedge into the self that splits us into the two sides of a coin. One side has the responsibility of improving the self; the other is the not-good-enough self that must be improved. As a result, rules, evaluation forms, and time sheets are a very important part of the positive thinking discourse, helping us to discipline and measure ourselves so that we can become someone who meets the expected standard and thus achieves more wealth.[57] Ehrenreich thinks this is why positive thinking doesn't help everyone. Instead, by constantly forcing us to think positively about everything, it ultimately leads to invisible pressure and emotional burnout, or even depression.

In *The Transparency Society*, Byung-Chul Han discusses how today's *society of positivity* tends to deny all *negative* things and emotions. We no longer have the ability to deal with pain and suffering, or even to give it form. In other words, love has become nothing more than one-dimensional consumption, something positive and comfortable that contains nothing distressing or negative.[58] Han considers truth a *negative force*; in the process of declaring everything else "false", it asserts itself. In contrast, *positivity* invariably rejects *negativity*; it encourages, asserts, and sings the praises of the current flow of information. But this cuts society off from the truth.[59]

In fact, a person's mental autonomy is frequently established only under conditions of negativity, and it is this very point which requires further discussion. For example, when a person reflects on ideas different from his or her own, or perhaps even receives an externally derived shock, it can sometimes result in a better understanding of the truth; conversely, if a person absorbs only information or ideas that *rationalize* or *agree with* their own thought processes, this affirmation is often just self-deception. This is perhaps the crux of positive thinking's danger: because it rejects any thought that makes us uncomfortable, such as life's darker aspects, it permits self-deception that results in self-constraint. In addition to this, Han reasons that the absence of external constraint in an achievement society does not indicate the absence of *any* constraint, only that the external constraint of negativity is turned into the internal constraint of positivity. He also suggests that Foucault's understanding of discipline might not apply to our present-day achievement society. This is because today constraint and discipline don't necessarily originate in systems external to the subject, as Foucault maintained, but are instead the subject's self-instituted constraints and norms.

I don't consider Han's point to be entirely correct, however. First of all, the discipline experienced by a subject in an achievement society still undergoes a shift from external to internal, after which it becomes external again, permitting others to imitate it. If it is the achievement-subject carrying out the violence of self-exploitation in a positive environment, then in a capitalist system such violence is often imitated and internalized by some achievement-model group. We see this in the self-improvement and positive thinking of our superiors or colleagues, who see that someone else appears to be doing quite well for themselves (receiving promotions and raises, for example), but do not see that person's unstable emotional state. Accordingly, it becomes "monkey see, monkey do" (the violence of the system having been unconsciously internalized). We therefore get a type of oppressive self-discipline that is first learned from a certain group and internalized as a form of self-constraint, and then influences others. As the performance of self-constraint intensifies, the entire group is pulled into a cycle of collective burnout.

We should not, however, ignore the *emotional labour* that is part of emotional capitalism, or as Maurizio Lazzarato calls it, the *immaterial labour*. This system-imposed worker exploitation is also quite common. The ability to voluntarily, freely express emotions is in fact good for human beings. If they feel offended, they can express their dissatisfaction with the offending person, or alternatively, they can show their sincere gratitude for someone's assistance. But in workplace environments where emotion cannot be expressed voluntarily, is unfree, or no choice is offered, the strict requirements of the work means workers go long periods of time unable to freely express their emotions, or that they put up an emotional facade (forcing a smile even if unhappy, for example). This is emotional alienation that constitutes violence toward and oppression of both body and mind. This is the problem of emotional labour.

In an early work of the sociologist Arlie Russell Hochschild, *The Managed Heart: Commercialization of Human Feeling*, she points out that the bulk of today's work is emotional labour carried out in the service industries. One example of this is flight attendants, who are trained in the skilful *inducement* and *suppression* of their emotions and facial expressions while serving guests.[60] Even if they are in a bad mood, they must be welcoming and accommodate customers with a smile. The forced emotions in such service work are in fact utterly exhausting and a form of emotional alienation. I think anyone who has worked in the service industry will know just how difficult it is. Under normal conditions, our care for others is reserved for those we like, but in today's world, it has been commercialized and turned into *hospitality* for guests who are strangers. Even if you don't like the other person, even if a customer complains or yells at you for poor service, you have to grin and bear it. Emotional workers have to endure it because this emotional mode of service (e.g., smiling) is part of the job.[61]

To create an atmosphere of heightened sensibility, an emotional capitalist society will often gamify the workplace and turn it into an affective space—restaurants will set themes for their decor (maid cafés are a good example) so that the server is no longer just a server, but an actor as well. That is, the server's clothing, tone of voice, and movements must all coordinate with the artificial surroundings and atmosphere. In addition, emotional industries often have *feeling rules* and scripts. These allow employees to self-assess their work performance[62] and make rigorous training an even greater necessity. As Hochschild points out, when airline attendants are trained, they are constantly reminded that they must keep smiling no matter what, that their smiles no longer theirs but company assets required to make a profit.[63] Thus, workers' bodies are the primary tool of emotional labour because it is only their bodies that can create consumer desire, and these workers only ever "play" a role of what appears to be "feeling".

The concept of emotional labour complements Marx's ideas of exploitation and alienation. Marx describes alienation as workers' inability to own the instruments of their labour, participate in the planning process, or own the products of their labour. Moreover, their labour power must also become an exchange value used to earn a wage and make their living. Inevitably, this type of exchange includes outsourcing one's emotions or turning them into emotional labour power which is then sold. For this reason, present-day emotional industries are a form of *institutional emotion management*[64] that demands emotions on the job be professionalized, normalized, and standardized, just like the training of professional actors. Staff at Disneyland, for example, must undergo training in emotional management, with their smiles subdivided according to degree. A smile cannot be totally unrestrained, but neither can it be insincere—if the smile is inappropriate, it could scare the children. People's emotions can't be tugged this way and that on just a whim, yet work requires them to fit their emotions to a model and a standard. And it is in fact this that makes the work so dehumanizing.

In the past, people who worked in factories were only required to sell their labour power and complete their work in a specified timeframe. Then they could leave work and collect their pay. (Even if they were in a bad mood that day, or were introverts not particularly adept at social interaction, they could simply keep their heads down and work hard.) Emotional capitalism, however, emphasizes the sale of not just a worker's physical labour to the workplace, but the body (physical self) and heart (emotional expression) as well. Both of these must align with the various *emotional images* corporations have established in the consumer space, to the extent that employees must even act out specific emotions in front of customers. These additional requirements exacerbate the difficulties of the workplace and bring about an alienation of emotions in addition to an alienation of labour. (In fact, the two types of alienation cannot be separated.) Since emotional labour often gives an advantage to extroverts good at controlling their emotions and social interactions, some introverts (such as those who are shy or have poor speaking skills) as well as people with poor emotional control (such as those with quick tempers) are at a disadvantage in emotionalized industry spaces. This is especially true in the service industry, where introverts and more reserved individuals are at a greater disadvantage when performing customer service jobs and so are more likely to receive customer complaints and reprimands from the boss. Such intangible qualities make it relatively difficult for people of a certain personality type to find a job in a capitalist society, even if he or she has other, less evident advantages (such as being detail-oriented or having excellent writing skills).

To borrow the terminology of French philosopher Bernard Stiegler, this is a process of *proletarianization*:[65] a capitalist, technological society constantly destroys and negates the worker's *savoir-faire* (their technical skill or know-how — because it is no longer needed in a commercial society) and *savoir-vivre* (knowledge of how to live).[66] Furthermore, their cognition and affect are completely altered to conform to the standards and logic of a consumer society. This is not only a process of re-*grammatization* (the *grammatization of gesture*) that uses a new logic of consumption (laughing or not laughing only under certain circumstances, for instance)[67] but has also become a *cognitive and affective proletarianization*.[68] For example, only a company's standards can be used to understand and respond to anything external; we must set aside any judgements of our own. The everyday operations of the libidinal economy have suppressed workers' lives so that an individual's libidinal energy is unable to freely develop and grow, thereby expanding life's horizons. Nor is an individual able to freely communicate with others and the external environment, which ultimately leads to being cut off from one's own life and existence.

Aside from this, the libidinal economy's most impressive aspect is its hyper-alertness to psychic energy *excess*. When it recognizes that an individual has become burned out through excessive work, it uses other methods to *repair* or *cure* the person's burned-out emotional state, either by permitting self-indulgence and release through consumer culture or by seeking to overcome the burned-out mental state through *pharmaceuticals* or *cognitive supplements*, thus giving the person renewed energy to deal with work. It's when some people don't enjoy combating the burnout with the "eat, drink, and be merry" or sensory indulgence approach (possibly the more they play, the more worn out they feel) that energy tonics and even sleeping pills start to play a major role. Laurent de Sutter has gone to the extent of using the term *narcocapitalism* to describe contemporary society. He points out that modern-day capitalism's greatest fear is people who suffer from stress-induced insomnia or poor sleep, because a worker who loses a night's sleep will be unable to work, which then results in decreased work efficiency. For this reason, drugs are used to assist (compel) sleep, to anaesthetize the body and mind, and ensure an individual is ready for work the next morning.[69] De

Sutter further notes what Marx already observed—that good sleep is key to the continuous production and reproduction of labour. This makes a peaceful night's sleep an important reason for establishing a capitalist social order, since a poor night's sleep is a predictor of less than maximal labour power.[70]

Because emotional capitalism's consumer culture industry might not always be able to relieve the burnout that work causes and may even intensify it, society has had to create the *mental health and health industries* that have become yet another set of profitable businesses. These industries include the *massage industry* to relieve physical fatigue (foot massages are available everywhere you go in Hong Kong); the *pharmaceutical industry* and *health industry* to look after our physical health; and the *counselling/psychotherapy industry* to see to our mental rehabilitation. All of these can be regarded as the self-healing function of the libidinal economy. As Han has pointed out, subjects today pursue personal health only to protect their bare lives as individuals, while the absolutization and fetishization of health has led us to see its value as an absolute that replaces theology with medical science. From a Nietzschean perspective, this is essentially *the last man*.[71]

Actually, I am in no way negating the importance of physical and mental health. However, no number of sleeping pills or psychologists will help if we become ill as a result of our failure to deal with insomnia and burnout (many illnesses stem from the accumulation of work-related exhaustion) or the underlying issue of massive systemic control (which can of course also be extended into efforts to improve the work environment and workers' welfare, e.g., the minimum wage). Nor will they help if the self fails to face up to or recognize the ideological manipulation of our mental landscape, with the result that individualization can no longer continue (such as when we pursue personal achievement at the expense of other values or connections in other areas of life), just as they won't help if we can no longer try to change the way we live or establish an alternative lifestyle (as, for instance, the many people today who devote themselves to assorted religious practices, farming, or running marathons, etc.).

As the American critic Christopher Lasch has concluded, if this pursuit of individual mental health is taken too far, it eventually breeds the narcissist's focus on feelings, well-being, health, and mental stability solely in terms of the self, or to a *therapeutic sensibility*, while a *retreat from politics* (or a self-absorbed complacency) leads to an interest solely in *psychic self-improvement* without any sense of historical belonging to connect past and future.[72] (Lasch is critiquing Americans of the 1970s, and though the situation then and now is of course quite different, his critique still has value; the narcissism he describes will only become worse, especially for the generations growing up with digital social media.) We shouldn't forget Freud's insight, which is that libido is always inclined towards self-attachment. Confronted with today's libidinal economy in combination with certain authoritarian countries, narcissists with this type of weak public spirit neither assume the responsibility of demanding social revolution nor transcend the self. Instead, they become quite politically conservative individuals. For a system that fears too many dissenting voices, it could even be said that this is exactly what the system wants. This is the reason that Han considers our current achievement society to be *a society of bare life*, in which everyone's purpose in life is merely to survive, rejecting any incursion of the other on the self. This type of life lacks psychopower and is no different than the life of a slave.[73]

The majority of Han's work helps us to see the relationship between an individual's emotions and capitalist society. Emotional capitalism controls our psychoemotional energy, thereby ensuring that capitalism can operate smoothly, but the smooth operation comes with the cost of producing one burned-out, depressed, and powerless subject after another. Eventually, it strips individuals of the ability to care about society or other people and becomes an emotional dictatorship. But in confronting this emotional dictator, how can we reverse course to transform our psyches and emotions and regain the ability to deal with others? Han offers almost no thoughts at all on this front. In the next chapter, the theories of Bernard Stiegler, Emmanuel Levinas, and Judith Butler will provide the framework for my attempt to locate an emotional ethics that responds to emotional capitalism and the emotional politics it creates.

Chapter 2

From the Burnout Subject to the Affective Subject: Bernard Stiegler on the Aesthetic Redemption of Spiritual Misery

Now, this misery or poverty is a disaffection, and the problem is thus to think how a disaffection affects me, and in what way I am already, myself, such a disaffected individual.

—Bernard Stiegler

The previous chapter discussed Byung-Chul Han's point that emotional capitalism acts as a libidinal economy, producing or managing libidinal energy and turning it into an instinctual emotional energy that serves capitalism. As a result, emotional capitalism produces self-exploiting achievement-subjects whose sole concern is individual achievement, ultimately leading to a life of exhaustion and depression. Emotional capitalism thus indirectly causes our preoccupation with self-care/treatment of our excess emotions, which in their transformed guise are no longer attuned to the needs of the other or to public affairs. But Han seems not to offer any path toward a solution for this dilemma. (He has always been more adept at raising an issue than solving it.) The contemporary French philosopher Bernard Stiegler, however, has also noted that libidinal capitalism leads to social and psychological problems. He then goes a step further, pointing out that such subjects are detached and *de-reasoning*; they are *disaffected individuals* who have no desire or motivation to connect with the other or to care about society.[74] But Stiegler does not simply point out the problem. He also offers possible solutions that would stop the war for control over affect/emotion in which we find ourselves.[75] One of these solutions is to retrain people's attention so that we develop the skills of looking carefully at objects as we silently observe them.[76] In this way, we can regain the emotional experience to which capitalist society has made us increasingly blind, and by redirecting libidinal energy toward the other and to new and different systems, use it to create and connect with new social systems.

Individuation of the Disaffected Subject

To understand Stiegler's concept of the disaffected individual first requires an understanding of the late French thinker Gilbert Simondon's theory of *individuation*. Stiegler was deeply influenced by Simondon, a technological philosopher who is now gaining increasing recognition despite his untimely passing in 1989, particularly in respect to his highly original ideas on the reciprocal shaping and symbiosis that takes place between humans and the technological environment. It is his ideas that have helped to establish a new philosophy and understanding of digital media. He states that human beings are not a fixed substance, and that the constant absorption of energy from an external (uncertain) milieu and other people brings about an individual's *becoming*.[77] This process of becoming is similar to what happens when a crystal forms, and requires a *germ* (seed) plus heat, pressure, polishing, the refraction of light, and chemistry; the form of something as it actually is and the potentiality of its matter are difficult to separate due to their complementary energies (although traditional forms of scholasticism say they can be differentiated). This is why form cannot be said to determine matter. Already-formed crystals will shape each other through external energy in the *structural milieu* (particularly because of germ-conferred energies) and will also constantly expand in all directions. In Simondon's view, a person's *becoming* therefore looks something like a *crystalline individual*. In the process of the individual linking to the preindividual milieu (a breeding ground that promotes becoming), there is a continuous accumulation of emotional energy, which is then kicked up a notch to another, still higher energy level. This is the process of individuation.[78] *Transindividuation* is the process of an individual's emotional/ affective energy expanding outwards: he or she transcends the self and connects both with other milieus and the emotions/ affect of the other. (These connections manifest as love and friendship.) An individual's additional expansion will even transform the milieu, allowing both it and the individual to continue in a mutual, prolific becoming that makes the form of life's existence highly dynamic and active.[79] In other words, Simondon places great value on the dominant role of *forces* in bringing together form and matter, these forces also being the intermediary that connects the individual to the external world.[80] Simondon's ideas can in fact be compared to this book's discussion of how the libidinal economy operates. Various types of psychic energy — such as libido, desire, and emotion — are linked to the various preindividual milieus of human beings (such as the technology milieu) and operate by supplementing or excluding one another, their existence due to the connections they are constantly making.

Inspired by Simondon's theory of individuation as outlined above, Stiegler's *disaffected individual* occurs when individuation is suppressed or disrupted by the culturally influenced technology consumption promoted by today's capitalism. (We don't think about anything except satisfying our individual desire to consume, for example, so that our sole motivation becomes a destructive desire.) This phenomenon is the process of *disindividuation*, in which the detached subject's connection with the collective/other is destroyed (i.e., I can't even take care of myself, so how can I help you!). Because the individual's libidinal energy (for Stiegler, libidinal energy is love[81]) cannot link with other individuals (love cannot be used to form a connection), the individual's energy does not rise to a new, higher level, and he or she is left incapable of forming a *we* relationship with the other. Ultimately, the individual is turned into a narcissist, with this narcissism constituting a psychological crisis for capitalism.[82] Human individuation, in the form of self-discovery or personal growth, for example, must therefore happen in a community where psychic energy is available. Anyone who withdraws from the community will have difficulty becoming a subject with a sense of responsibility.

Of course, Stiegler also points out that there is not just a disruption of psychic energy, but also of knowledge acquisition, referring here to the two types of knowledge that existed before the capitalist market: know-how (*savoir faire*) and knowledge of how to live (*savoir vivre*).[83] Because entering the capitalist market requires the worker to give up the know-how he or she already possesses (such as knowledge of how to farm) in order to accommodate the exclusive know-how and technological processes of production in a capitalist technological society (like the mechanized technology depicted in Chaplin's *Modern Times*), an alienation of knowledge results. The worker is trapped in a predicament of *proletarianization* or *disindividuation*, no longer able to live by relying on his or her own skill. Workers therefore lead helpless lives, like the farmer whose agricultural skills are rarely used in an industrialized and digitized society; and even when such rarely used skills can be put to use, it's difficult to make a living from them. Since know-how is no longer useful, people no longer have any interest in sharing their skills with others or with the next generation, and as a result even *life* knowledge is lost. Ultimately, everyone turns their lives over to consumption and the technological society, which accelerates proletarianization.

In addition to this proletarianization and disindividuation, capitalist society is constantly undergoing *processes of technical exteriorization*, meaning that technology systems are now our stand-ins for every conceivable life skill. This extends even into *mnemotechnologies* (such as drawing and writing to make a record of things). These basic life technologies are subject to the control of what Stiegler calls the *industrialization of human memory and cognition*. They add additional pressure for people to give up their knowledge of how to live and switch to using the skills and knowledge approved by a capitalist and technological society. This all-pervasive, systemic replacement of human technologies with technological systems and thinking has led to a *spiritual misery*, caused the suppression and failure of our psychic, collective, and social individuation processes,[84] and made us detached from the human spirit and knowledge. In short, it has become a matter of *sociopathology*.[85]

When know-how and knowledge of how to live are replaced by consumer and financial information, people become so interested in it that end up overloaded by an excess of inanimate online information. The result is an *emotional/cognitive saturation* that ultimately leads to a *disaffected individual*, someone who has no feelings about life.[86] I would like to add, however, that Stiegler's emotional saturation is also the sense of being emotionally powerless that is caused by emotional capitalism-induced exhaustion. To be *disaffected* probably does not mean being impassive, but to no longer care about the needs of the external world or the other. In a burnout society, people live only inside their own feelings and care only about their own future with no concern for the external world. Superficially, this state of being is also a type of individuation in that it is similar to the subject's self expansion (or *self-exploitation*, as previously discussed in relation to Byung-Chul Han). In fact, however, it is Stiegler's deindividuation, because the person has not made self-enhancing and life-transforming connections with an external other.

Stiegler is not concerned with the individual development of the liberated subject; he is instead worried about our lives and knowledge being subject to a system of consumer goods and technology—what he calls a *hypermarket*—leaving us unable to connect with the other or civic society. Stiegler is not a conservative, anti-technology thinker, of course. He uses the term *pharmakon* to describe technology as both destructive and curative, as either *poison or medicine*. Which one it is depends on how we use technology systems to accelerate the development of new psychic and collective individuation. An individual is expanded by technology but can also internalize technology in a *process of exteriorization-interiorization*.[87] But influenced by the hypermarket, our public life—a sense of a collective *we*—has been destroyed. Stiegler gives the example of today's parents, who don't know how to love the next generation or pass on their life knowledge to them. This is not because the parents of today are bad people, but because we often ask consumer society to do these things for us, such as when we buy our children something as a substitute for love.

To love, however, is not just the consumption of feelings. It is also a relationship, a way of existing that extends to the smallest detail of the knowledge of how to live.[88] Unfortunately, in today's consumer society, products have replaced parents and become the objects with which their children identify. Our emotional lives have now entered an age of *emotional contracting*.[89] In some Asian countries like Hong Kong or Singapore, our children's emotional and life educations have been outsourced to foreign domestic helpers. This has severed our connection to the next generation, and even resulted in their feelings of despair and anxiety. (In fact, I find that many children today are prone to anxiety, and that this is caused not just by education-related stress, but also their lack of problem-solving abilities. This may be the long-term result of parents delegating their children's daily lives to foreign domestic helpers.) This is a problem in today's emotional consumer society that requires our careful attention.

Stiegler worries that once everyone has become detached from the things around them, the hypermarket will eventually destroy the emotional community, which is an ethically political social unit that accommodates emotional exchange and shared spaces.[90] What Stiegler is concerned about is the dissolution of ethical life, the loss of love, and the demise of justice,[91] by which he means the loss of *collective desires* (friendship, respect, self-esteem). Without love, there is no motivation to live an ethical life. But of even greater importance is that emotional apathy and burnout make people numb to injustice, so that they no longer experience distress on behalf of those who are suffering or even think about them. More recently, academics such as Peter Sloterdijk have asserted that, aside from a culture of competition, rage is all that's left to us in a capitalist society dominated by neo-liberalism. The recent sense of fatigue pervading Hong Kong society stems from more than just the emotional labour and consumption that are depleting our emotional lives; it is increased by an across-the-board disappointment with politicians, political parties, and the government since the 1997 Handover. Add to this a feeling of powerlessness after multiple unsuccessful large-scale protest movements, and the result is exhaustion and a loss of hope that individuals can bring about any type of social reform. Once all hope is lost, we are ultimately left only with populism. As Stiegler said, an individual's *demotivation* in regard to public reform can be blamed on mediocre politicians, in that noncaring detachment also means a loss of political critical spirit.[92]

Stiegler also sees today's capitalist society as an example of Deleuze's *control society*, which reduces morality to the law and then uses "illegality" to round up and reform dissenters at every turn. But I would also add that we live in a *surveillance society* that uses lightning-fast, no-place-to-hide surveillance technology to control every move people make; it also uses the pretext of gathering consumer credit data to record people's lives, behaviour, and habits. In this way, capitalism controls and disciplines us, governing us by producing a state of fear (anyone who doesn't conform may be prosecuted or even imprisoned). People's social lives are filled with panic and uneasiness, accelerating their detachment from society and public affairs. Such occurrences are already common in today's post-pandemic state.

Emotional Experience Reshaped by Aesthetics

How then should we restore feeling for the other? How do we change disaffected individuals into their opposite? In *Symbolic Misery, Volume 1: The Hyperindustrial Epoch*, Stiegler suggests that aesthetics have this redemptive potential. For Stiegler, aesthetics is first and foremost an experience of sensing or perception that is related to and inseparable from politics.[93] He points out that the current aesthetic crisis is not their absence but a narrowing of our options to just one: the commoditized, popular aesthetics of a hypercapitalist society, which fails to demonstrate any characteristic specific to the individual. He also points out that control societies have turned aesthetics into digital technologies that use our conscious and unconscious rhythms to control us body and soul; our lives and feelings do not originate in us but are instead created by a commodity society. This aesthetic disindividuation is a garbage aesthetics with no spiritual value, one that is ultimately unable to establish a common aesthetic experience so that we are able to regain our *sense of "we"* and face up to the other.[94]

At first glance, Stiegler's observations appear to be nothing new. The Frankfurt School pointed out the aesthetic crisis precipitated by mass commodity culture before Stiegler did, and the problem of aesthetic forms and their autonomy also preoccupied the German philosopher Theodor W. Adorno. Stiegler, however, has given greater time and attention than the Frankfurt School to the study of mass consumer goods produced by aesthetic technologies, with a particular focus on the control and manipulation of human affect. This led him to the concepts of *organology*, his three-stranded, transdisciplinary research into human sense organs, artificial technical organs, and social organizations;[95] it also led him away from a critical analysis based on the macroscopic ideology of traditional political economy. As a result, Stiegler is more attentive to the body and emotions than traditional political economy, and (with the exception of Marcuse) more microscopic and detailed in his analysis.

Stiegler considers the biggest problems of commodity aesthetics/beauty to be the *symbolic misery* that results from it and its destruction of our emotional world. That is, the cultural signs and information (or the emotional consumption of commodity signs) that capitalism gives us are simply a bunch of signs without spiritual value, used to entice us into the world of consumer goods. But our emotional world is eventually dominated by the standardized aesthetics that cookie-cutter merchandise produces, and in addition to totally sublimating and transforming individual growth, such standardization doesn't permit human beings to create *singularities* or to make art. From the point commodity aesthetics takes hold, we no longer have the ability or technology to independently create art, and the only "feelings" available for us to use are those the culture industry provides. We rarely paint a picture or write a poem to express our sorrow; instead, we opt for karaoke, expressing ourselves by singing along with technology-produced "sorrow", ultimately putting the opportunities to express our own lives and our ability to deal with objects/the world/the other into someone else's hands.

Art gives people a singular but not necessarily unique experience, and this is precisely what Stiegler considers important. A singular experience is first-person; it is the subject's *sensibility*, or perception of and acute responsiveness to his or her relationship with the world (such as when we make a painting to express our concerns about life). An artwork's uniqueness does not necessarily guarantee such a first-person perceptual experience, however. (Artworks or objects that I did not create, no matter how unique, remain someone else's experience.) Some works of art are even copied and mass-produced, which turns them into commodified signs.

Stiegler gives even greater attention to the problem of memory, which in a consumer society is superseded by and stored in digital technologies to produce an identical *collective memory*. This is not to say that we don't spontaneously remember by our very nature (*primary memory*), or that what determines our ability to store memories is not our genes (*secondary memory*); these are what Stiegler calls *genetic memory* and *epigenetic memory*. But in today's fully technicalized society, there is also *epiphylogenetic memory* (or *tertiary memory*). This is a *technical* memory system external to our physical selves, such as the On This Day memories that Facebook calls up and presents each day. These memories, however, are the carefully filtered, organized memories handed to us by a high-speed, large-volume data system in a process that fractures people's relationships with their own memories. Alternatively, consider the digital photo storage systems everyone uses today. Our photos are no longer displayed in our homes to be fully appreciated as they were in the past; instead, we keep thousands of pictures in our digital storage systems and quickly forget all about them. There is no accumulation of surplus emotion, and even the historical experience that connects generations is ruptured.

Stiegler's greatest concern is that tertiary memory has outstripped the other two types so that human cultural heritage (including the use of objects), everyday life knowledge, and artistic creation will no longer come from personal experience or the technical skills learned from using objects. (Martin

Heidegger expressed such skills as *tekhne*, a Greek word meaning *craftsmanship* and not just *high technology* as it does today.) That is, knowledge will no longer come from physical interaction with objects (as Heidegger says, humans must use an object before they can know its existential meaning and its value for the *I*), which is what humans use to develop a shared living memory. (In the Agricultural Age, farmers shared their knowledge of solutions to agricultural problems, improved techniques, and so on, evolving a culture that was passed down from one generation to the next.)

Electronic memory technologies are used as a *prosthesis* that helps humans to live their lives, yet take away the opportunities human beings have to share, communicate, and recall their actual emotions and experiences by creating art. Ultimately, human historical memory is simply a hybrid constructed by an artificial *technical prosthesis*. The original, historical memory is lost, creating a human existence in which things are deleted and forgotten. Chinese scholar Zhang Yibing notes that the comprehensive rational ability which constitutes subjectivity is entirely short-circuited in Stiegler's description of epiphylogenetic memory:

People's reason for being and ability to survive (for instance, how we view and make changes to the world, how we choose to live, which products we purchase, etc.) are no longer truly a matter of our own cognition, nor even a function of society's overall culture and knowledge, but rather the standards and methods generated by huge volumes of data external to people and external to social being. This is most likely the fundamental cause of the social subject's systemic ignorance.[96]

Of course, this is more than just the basis for systemic ignorance. It also marks the start of humans forfeiting memory.

Influenced by the ideas of anthropologist André Leroi-Gourhan, Stiegler believes that art, handcrafted objects (such as bowls), and performance (such as dance) have the function of shaping community identity and empathy. This shaping is based not just on the art's materiality and symbolism but also on its rhythmicality, with the human body and its five senses playing an important intermediary role. As technology has developed, however, it has gradually begun to handle and even control this aesthetic sensibility formerly produced with our bodies, so that members of the community increasingly lack knowledge of or are no longer interested in using their technical skills in daily life, let alone using them to create a communal aesthetic experience and historical memory. (People today are more interested in the stories told by Netflix's movies than in oral history or stories about their own communities.) This state of affairs eventually destroys the community's unique *sensible* experience. It also indirectly causes our lack of interest in others and the community. Aside from our loss of sensibility, we no longer have any ability to use signs and our knowledge of how to live to present our own/others' stories and lives (such as by creating our own stage play), and so to some lesser or greater degree, we become disaffected from public life. This is not to say that personal experience can be transmitted only through what someone creates; some members of the community will always have greater artistic talent or creative resources than others. What matters is whether these individuals can create something for community members, especially something that faithfully expresses and interprets life experiences and feelings, rather than just satisfy market demand.

I would like to add that the *structure of feeling* present in today's emotional capitalism is not derived from the interactions of community members in (daily) life, but from a collective feeling produced by digital media technology. The latter no longer encourages human beings to spontaneously develop or arrive at a set of cultural signs, which are rooted in the emotion, cognition, spirit, and ethics of human life and stored in individual memory, and so people eventually fall into the weakened state Stiegler calls the *loss of symbolic participation*. Empty and utilitarian market logic and signs are all that remain, and it is these that control human desire, emotion, cognition, and memory, these that eliminate the possibility of individuated development and bring about a crisis of deindividuation[97] as life evolves into an absence of feeling for the world and other people.[98]

Accordingly, Stiegler believes that an *artisanal* approach to art and creative output—art that can express the emotional life of an individual is the only way we can put people back in touch with the world and the other. (I will use *tea ceremony culture* to discuss this further in the next section.) He considers this type of aesthetics vital in that creative expression can bring about a turn toward a new community sensibility and shape an awareness of an *us* or *we*.[99] This is reminiscent of the artwork and songs with messages of democracy and freedom that Umbrella Movement and anti-extradition protest demonstrators in Hong Kong spontaneously created to unite people, protest the government, and mourn those who suffered for the movements, thereby establishing shared emotion. It is this *we*, manifested through art, that acts as a unified consciousness.[100] Stiegler's aesthetic thought is not, therefore, apolitical. He stressed that a group cannot become a true political community in the absence of any shared feeling, or if they have nothing about which they care deeply that will bring them together, such as values, language, the landscape, or their city. Just as a community can't operate without having some feeling or desire in common, neither can this common feeling be achieved if the people don't create their own art.[101] Naturally, this kind of aesthetic experience and its accompanying symbolic signs require a keen awareness of some social injustice that manifests as a predicament of human honour and shame. Only then can a relationship of shared cares truly be established between an individual and the other.

Ethical Experience Reshaped by Attention

In a consumer society, the sole emphasis is on consumption and disposables; we are not encouraged to value objects. Stiegler therefore suggests we rediscover object *fidelity*. By creating a *transitional space* from a single, fixed object, we can reorganize and channel our psychic energy, thereby transforming a *narcissistic drive* into the motivation and desire to change society.[102] In his book *What Makes Life Worth Living*, Stiegler borrows the idea of a *transitional object* from the psychologist D.W. Winnicott. Stiegler explains that these objects, which might be a Teddy bear or a blanket, create a strong link between child and parent. They establish the parent's care, allowing the child to derive trust, warmth, love, and hope from the item. In other situations, objects can serve as intermediaries in the social communications and relations people establish with the other, while caring/solicitous relationships may even be constituted of certain objects.[103] Such relationships are not based solely on the drive to consume goods but are also expressions of love and care for the other's libido, shown via the objects. Unfortunately, in an age of overconsumption where consumer culture means there is little encouragement to cherish anything, object *infidelity* makes it difficult to reconstruct a social transitional space in which love (*philia*), loyalty, and care predominate.

Objects can be the making of a person. Alternatively, they can destroy a person. Which of these occurs depends on whether the individual sees an object's *transitionality* or *limitedness*. If this is not seen, an otherwise free person becomes subservient to the object or addicted to it as a plaything. Anymore, we are the servants of consumer goods, and therefore the attention we give objects is not about rejecting or accepting them, but our perception of them as a kind of medicine.[104] As medicine, they are both helpful and harmful, destructive and redemptive, depending on how people envision, use, and understand them and thus find life's value in them. This line of thought that critiques ordinary objects as both poison and medicine, and which Stiegler showers with admiration, is known as *pharmacology*. But how do we rediscover the redemptive nature of objects? Stiegler believes that to *coindividuate*, we must learn to give objects our sustained attention and *discernment*. Our interaction and integration with the external world (the world/ the other) thereby counteract consumer society's excessive speed and its destruction of objects' humanistic and spiritual value.

Stiegler's way of putting thin is somewhat abstract. As I see it, this *transitional space* formed from a *transitional object* is similar to the Japanese tea ceremony culture. In the Japanese novel *Every Day a Good Day*, the author Noriko Morishita writes about a young woman who learns the proper procedure for making tea, guided by her tea ceremony teacher. She attentively and patiently fixes her gaze on the tea ware and utensils as she completes each step of the ceremony according to the required timing. Through her physical and emotional use of the tea ware, tea aroma, and other transitional objects, the tea maker senses the world's seasonal flow as well as how the objects connect to her own experience and understanding of life, and she uses this sensibility to construct a humanistic space. (The object functions exactly like a geometric "solid" formed by a series of geometric points, meaning that it forms a space that both is and is not a space, both there and not.) In this way, she discovers all that life has to offer. This is a process of *transindividuation*, in which the individual is not a servant to the object but instead the recipient of a fulfilling and uplifting experience. In a practice like this, the subject is affected by objects yet remains in constant connection with the external world through them. The result is a life-enriching experience that may be a viable way of responding to the spiritual crisis brought about by contemporary emotional capitalism.

For this reason, Stiegler places particular stress on our (especially young people's) need for contemplation (what the Greeks called *skhole*) in the form of *attention, somatic techniques, and psychotechniques*.[105] This means we concern ourselves with only one thing at a time and focus our *deep attention* on a single object.[106] (Of course, a situation in which the subject's first physical experience is something unique, original, and formative is very much influenced by Husserl's phenomenology.) This type of attention resists easy distraction yet lacks the persistent, fixed quality of *hyperattention*. Learning how to do this is a lot like the child who goes to school for the first time and must be trained how to learn—how to sit and pay attention, how to ask questions, how to remember, how to interact with others—before any actual content can be taught.[107] For Stiegler, attention is a type of contemplation. As Husserl put it, it is the operational arrangement between *retentions* (memory) and *protentions* (anticipation).[108] The difference between humans and animals lies in the former's ability to settle into a lasting *psychic faculty* by giving their attention to an object, which enables the human to wait quietly while reorganizing emotions/desires/awareness. (Stiegler also suggested a mindful stroll down the street, reading, and writing[109] as ways of establishing a concern for and pleasure in objects or things.[110]) The result is a transitional space,[111] a consumer space unlike the one that simply creates greed for the new while casting aside and forgetting the old. This space allows the free operation of emotion/desire/knowledge and enables connection with the other. (The Hong Kong Umbrella Movement's occupied zone, religious sites, and community classrooms are examples of this type of transitional space.) The transitional space can help the subject shed the mindset of seeing the things around him or her as irrelevant or pointless[112] and establish a community of *you and me* by displaying his or her concern for people, objects, and things.

In the famous Japanese comic, *Midnight Diner*, the chef only uses food to stimulate the memories of emotionally wounded people and bring healing into their lives. Food becomes a transitional object used as a tool rather than an object to be consumed, the diner is transformed from a consumer space into a life-building and curative/transitional space, and as a result, the emotionally wounded patrons can feel that life is worth living. We may be parts in the system, but we do not have to be identical cogs in it, driven to total despair. Avoiding such despair depends on our willingness to attempt to produce the psychic energy that can resist or disrupt capitalism's discipline. With that energy, we can establish new systems, *long circuits of attention*, and space in which people can engage in emotional exchange.

By Stiegler's criteria, the chef in *Midnight Diner* and the tea ceremony teacher in *Every Day a Good Day* are ideal artistic personae. For Stiegler, artists should pursue individuation (a rich, full life) as well as be people who promote individuation. How an artist attends to symbols, how personal singularities of feeling and time show up during this process, as well as the connections an artist makes with the community to which he/she belongs and with the other's feelings and time—these are what permit the interactions between individual and collective that establish shared memory. It is through this shared memory that individuals resist being shaped by the systems of cultural industry, capitalism, and the state, in addition to the external memories that have been imposed on the public and do not belong to them. (Stiegler uses *hypersynchronization* to critique this type of cultural industrial production and its *toxic* mass memory and time.) Subsequently, life as a *you and me* community is encouraged. Art is therefore not a purely personal and private activity, nor at all narcissistic, but has a psychosocial aspect. In this regard, Stiegler, inspired in particular by the German artist Joseph Beuys's *social sculpture* of last century, believes that the popular aesthetics and sensibility we are gradually losing must be reconstituted to combat the problematic commercialization of art.[113]

A particular point Stiegler makes is that artists should help make it possible for people to look closely at the same artwork for a long, uninterrupted period through an aesthetics of *repetition*, or that their repetitive artistic creations should contain variations.[114] (An example of the latter would be the improvisation found in jazz music, where notes are actually rearranged to make the same song different each time it is performed.) Each time an artwork is viewed, the viewer will discover that changes in the self will cause him or her to sense a new *I* being formed during the process of individuation.[115] Every repetition is life being enriched, thereby keeping at bay the culture industry's monotonous aesthetics, which have been created by an aesthetics of speed and neglect the individual. This is why, as previously described, the tea ceremony teacher helped her audience to engage in a repetitive contemplation of the tea ware, and thus create the life of an artist. In this way, too, the chef in *Midnight Diner*, who cooks the food customers like again and again, helps his customers to re-establish their memories of and relations with the individual and the other, guiding them through the process of enriching each other's lives.

Stiegler believes that it's better for such artists to be amateurs. Because amateurs have not been fully absorbed into the culture industry, they have also absorbed far less of its poison, and as a result, they can practise and cultivate an aesthetics that runs counter to that of the culture industry, doing so with earnestness, enthusiasm, and love. This opposite approach is of course the previously mentioned aesthetics of repetition, which emphasizes contemplation and life insights. Such an approach may well be the role of public intellectuals in today's emotional capitalist society – although not just the traditional public intellectuals. Edward Said has suggested that these individuals must provide *marginal* perspectives and become political dissidents inducted into the ranks of those fighting the system. It is now also even more necessary for us to further cultivate people's libidinal and psychic energies, to resist proletarianization, to help people re-establish their lost know-how and knowledge of how to live. In practising this aesthetic, amateur contemplators/artists are producing psychic energy that responds to the world's needs.

Such thinking has greatly broadened our picture of intellectuals, especially those who have begun to resist capitalism's control through their physical or spiritual practice. Some of the protestors involved in Hong Kong's recent social movements, for example, have used the repetition of daily agricultural work as a way of building up their will to resist and to create an alternative lifestyle. Even some religious practitioners have sought a spiritual foundation for resistance in repetitive daily practice. If *repetition* is a kind of constant practice (this is in fact the word's meaning in French[116]), then artists are practitioners, and only through a near-religious practice that demands their patient contemplation of objects will the disaffected be able to reattune to their emotions and so be affected by love. (Stiegler has even suggested that through slowness, quietness, and solitude, a person can return to his or her original emotional state.[117])

But make no mistake. Far from being an idealist, Stiegler has simply made human inner consciousness and emotional practice his focus. He believes that technology cannot be substituted for human perception and memory, or we will be rendered incapable of constructing an affective, ethical experience of the world and the other. Nor has he neglected the importance of establishing new systems. From the beginning, his hope has been that a new, contribution-style economic model could be established. The basis of this model would be the real need for the production of goods rather than the false need produced by the consumer culture economic model, so that innovative technologies no longer serve the consumer-goods market but people in need. In an attempt to develop new companies and make possible the cross-industry collaborative research that will change the orientation of consumer desire, Stiegler brought together engineers, programmers, economists, and philosophers to establish Ars Industrialis and the Institut de Recherche et d'Innovation (IRI) in France. In response to the ecological crisis caused by the Anthropocene,[118] for example, these organizations developed non-profit freeware. From this it is clear that Stiegler advocates a redemptive style of capitalism, a style likewise represented by his development of *organology*, which links the human sense organs, artificial technical organs, and social organizations. As we respond to emotional capitalism (Stiegler did not use this term, although the problems he saw certainly resulted from it), his ideas could provide us with a more redemptive strategy.

Chapter 3

From the Affective Subject to the Ethical Subject: Emmanuel Levinas on the Inseparability of Suffering from the Ethics of the Other

The more I return to myself, the more I divest myself, under the traumatic effect of persecution, of my freedom as a constituted, willful, imperialist subject, the more I discover myself to be responsible; the more just I am, the more guilty I am. I am "in myself" through the others.

— Emmanuel Levinas

Whether we are discussing the burnout-subject of Byung-Chul Han or the disaffected subject of Bernard Stiegler, the individual is emotionally numb and indifferent to the exterior world. This disaffected subject has neither the motivation to communicate with and help others nor any interest in establishing an intersupportive sense of community (Stiegler's ethical sense of *we*). In fact, the predicament we face today is an ever-greater ignorance of and disdain for the living conditions of the other. From Syrian refugees to the Rohingya in Myanmar, from unskilled labourers in Mainland China to Hong Kong's poor, all these examples of the other have had their right to life exploited. The Italian political philosopher Roberto Esposito believes that to protect their members from invasion by outsiders, today's communities are increasingly seeing themselves as groups with immunity;[119] The other, who belongs to a group foreign to the community, is accordingly eliminated like a germ and subjected to violent treatment (such as when refugees are dragged out of the high seas). In addition to this, we are seeing present-day capitalism in combination with the state carry out a daily increase in the manipulation, surveillance, and segregation of the public. Add to this the serious problem of human exploitation that occurs in emotional labour, and we are inevitably even more on guard against the suffering and oppressed other. For this reason, contemporary Western theorists are rethinking various biopower systems and how violence plays an implicit or explicit role in our treatment of the life of the other. Giorgio Agamben, for example, critiques national forms of government that use *a state of exception*[120] to strip a person of all rights, creating one *bare life* after another. Zygmunt Bauman describes *liquid modernity* and reflects on the *wasted lives* that cannot keep up with its high rate of productivity and consumption; he also demonstrates that contemporary theorists are right to ask how the state incorporates capitalism and constructs/plans/manages our subjectivity and the extent to which we value life.

As we face our current predicament, we should not be concerned solely with how those in power dominate and oppress the other. We should also take an interest in how we can transform the individuals of a civil society from indifferent subjects into affective subjects who care about others; in how a disaffected subject can regain the power to rebel and even how to nurture subjects who become the other in order to protest. I don't deny the need to change the system. The system must be changed to change the lives of the vulnerable. But this cannot be done all at once. The only things we can change as we quietly await opportunities for reform are people's opinions, lives, and even libidinal energy. As discussed in the previous chapter, Stiegler's *pharmacological critique* of objects, power, desire, and technology is one way for us to examine capitalism during its current crisis and inspect its state of health, to critique life-destroying consumer desire, and to redistribute our libidinal energy (love) through practices that link the other into a new system of economics. Stiegler certainly sees libidinal love (a love for the community) as a force that promotes reform, yet the left, right, and various nationalisms of today are using the vocabulary of *love* to promote their own political projects. How can we guarantee that love's emotional power is not just an excuse to carry out violence against the other? How do we ensure that Stiegler and Simondon's *coindividuation*—a state in which the psychopower of both parties proves to be mutually enriching—is not simply a different kind of subject annexing the other? For instance, in Hong Kong, the groups of "Hong Kong patriots" that have appeared in the city in recent years are premised solely on the calculation of naked self-interest. They suppress freedom and diversity in the name of "love for the city" and seek homogeneity. As for the right wing political groups that are "anti-foreign", the only love they accept is conditional, and so they become a *we* in the very narrowest sense.

In their book *Multitude*, Antonio Negri and Michael Hardt contend that when the global power order is based on violence and war, the subject should rely on love to accomplish a genuinely revolutionary cause. They believe that despite love having been previously understood as a private emotion shared by couples or nuclear families, we should look to the pre-modern Jewish and Christian religions for a public and political love and use this to develop the political action of the multitude[121] — we should gather the multitude with love, not hate—and so bring true justice and peace to society. Negri has even said that "without this love, we are nothing."[122]

But Negri and Hardt overlook that political resistance requires a certain ethical motivation extrinsic to the subject. More specifically, it must promote a nonviolent politics in which the other takes precedence. It must first compel the subject to be responsible for the other, which then leads to an ethical biopolitics based on the other. Although Negri and Hardt note that the ethical subject is also love's affective subject, they overlook that the other can be a source of affective energy and rely too much on the spontaneity and self-discipline of the subject in social action.

In his book *Infinitely Demanding*, the British philosopher Simon Critchley points out that "politics is not the naked operation of power or an ethics-free agonism, it is an ethical practice that is driven by a response to situated injustices and wrongs."[123] Critchley's starting point is Jewish thinker Emmanuel Levinas's *ethics of the other*. He takes Levinas's thought a step further, however, pointing out that the subject is necessarily an individual responsible only for the life of the other, one who has no loyalties to any political system and who will always insist on *dissensus*. This is an *anarchic subject* who constantly opposes and criticizes the regime or *totality of the state* oppressing the other.[124]

More importantly, Levinas's ethical subject does not exercise a responsibility derived from abstract laws or the subject's free will, but from the other's suffering and grief, which transforms the subject from indifferent disaffection to an affective state. As Critchley points out:

> In grief and mourning we undergo an experience of affective self-dispossession or self-undoing that can provide the motivational force to enter into a political sequence.[125]

This is why, having taken a close look at numerous contemporary theorists' ideas on the subject, including those of Alain Badiou, Lacan, and Levinas, Critchley confirms that Levinas's ethical subject is not only the most capable of practising non-violent action, but can also respond responsibly to the *infinite demand* of the other. This is because Levinas's other is able to transcend the subject while also restraining the subject's egoism, being an ethical force derived from the body and emotions that does not fall into Lyotard's ethics-discarding libidinal politics.[126]

When we consider how to transform a disaffected subject into an affective subject, I still think there must be a suffering other who transcends the subject, and that aside from serving as the extrinsic motivation which helps the subject to escape his or her indifference, the vulnerability of this suffering other also has the potential to suppress the subject's violent tendencies. In the following section, I will discuss in greater depth Levinas's ethics of the other with particular emphasis on the power of emotional ethics, which I believe will assist in establishing an ethics of emotional politics.

The Ethics of the Other Generated by Suffering

Levinas was a phenomenologist born in Lithuania in 1906. In his younger years, he studied at the University of Freiburg, where he attended Husserl's lectures and benefitted from Heidegger's instruction. During the Second World War, Levinas's parents and younger brother died in a concentration camp. He was detained in a prisoner of war camp and so avoided a similar fate. After the war, his experience of the Nazis drove him to reconsider the Western philosophical tradition, the entirety of which, from ancient Greece to the modern era, had been based on ontology and the cognizing subject. He reflected on how violence was given form and ignited by disregard for the other, which had created the conditions for the Holocaust. As he says, can we still talk about an absolute moral law after Auschwitz (a Nazi concentration camp located in southern Poland)? Can we talk about morality after morality has failed?[127]

Levinas's important works are *Totality and Infinity* and *Otherwise than Being or Beyond Essence*. The former focuses on the ethical characteristics of the other, while the latter gives greater attention to the question of ethical subjectivity. In *Totality and Infinity*, Levinas argues that human beings always have egoistic tendencies until they encounter the other. A person's duty to others occurs only in situations that are passive and unfree, and the subject takes responsibility for the other only after he or she experiences the shock of being confronted with the other's suffering face. Levinas further points out that the Western intellectual tradition (intellectualism) is a tradition of *egology*[128] that has always revered the subject's reason and consciousness and pursues only the *self-sufficiency of the same*.[129] It is a tradition that has ignored difference and bestowed rationality and consciousness on the subject while maintaining a sure priority (priority of the subject) when apprehending things external to itself. Philosophy is the love of wisdom. But as a Jewish thinker, Levinas believes that "philosophy is the wisdom of love at the service of love."[130] He attempts to use the Hebrew tradition of love only (also a tradition of peace [*shalom*])[131] to revise the wisdom-only tradition of Greece and Rome, substituting the priority of the subject with the priority of the other and replacing the activity of the subject with passivity, which ultimately transforms the rational and disaffected knowledge-seeking subject into an affective ethical subject.

In his monumental work *Totality and Infinity*, Levinas first makes the very astute point that "Western philosophy has most often been an ontology: a reduction of the other to the same by the interposition of a middle and neutral term that ensures the comprehension of being."[132] This seemingly neutral system of comprehending conceals its internal power operations, however. Accordingly, Levinas also points out that Western philosophers from the Greeks to the Enlightenment and up to and including Heidegger's phenomenology have regarded ontology as the first philosophy[133] — a philosophy of power — and that a highly abstract *thematization* and *conceptualization*[134] have played a major role in how these philosophers have constructed the essence of being/existence for humans and the world. But while ontology satisfies the subjective consciousness of the other and of being, violence is built into it. In its pursuit of sameness, it classifies and conceptualizes an other not easily made the same or categorized and uses the *totalizing power of reason* to destroy corporeality, variation, and alterity. In doing so, it more easily establishes a general knowledge of human beings, which ultimately satisfies the subject's metaphysical desire to manipulate the other and the world. For Levinas, ontology is overall a philosophy of injustice.[135]

A Holocaust survivor, Levinas also points out that it was this type of ontology that constituted the Nazis' Holocaust logic and their treatment of Jews. In *Difficult Freedom*, Levinas explains:

Political totalitarianism rests on an ontological totalitarianism. Being is all, a Being in which nothing finishes and nothing begins. Nothing stands opposed to it, and no one judges it. It is an anonymous neuter, an impersonal universe, a universe without language.[136]

This dehumanizing ontology places the disembodied other into a conceptual knowledge system, which later becomes an excuse for totalitarians/racists (such as Adolf Hitler) to carry out collective violence against the other. In fact, the only thing racists need to do to rationalize their hatred is to assign a supposedly innate or biologically inferior nature to an other from a different race and then apply this idea with biopolitical universalism. (The Nazis, for example, regarded the Jews scattered across Europe as "hybrids" and "germs" who had no clear national identity. Because this had an effect on the social order of German society at that time, they could therefore rationalize the elimination of Jews as impurities.)

As a result, Levinas not only considers Western philosophers who regard ontology or knowledge as the first philosophy to be incorrect but believes that modernity's various types of collective violence are the result of a gene created by this point of view. He points out that the Western tradition of subjective philosophy has always turned a blind eye to the other, who has not been permitted an active role in shaping the subject's ethical character, and also that, for the sake of knowledge, this tradition has failed to suppress the subject's potential for violence, so that the subject ultimately becomes disaffected. Levinas wants not just to incorporate the other, but also to make the forming of subjectivity conditional upon the other—that is, subjective responsibility is assigned by the other rather than determined by the subject's reason. This totally undoes the violent nature of the rational subject who uses knowledge to oppress the other, and it is this idea to which Levinas gives special attention in his second major work, *Otherwise than Being or Beyond Essence*.

But if the subject's ability to think rationally should not have priority during contact with the other, which physical ability should? If ontology is not the first philosophy, which philosophy is? Levinas believes ethics should be the first philosophy, not the ontology that Western intellectual tradition has long admired. The ethics to which he refers, however, is not Kant's universal moral law, but an extra-legal, Other-oriented, intersubjective physical relation. This type of ethics is a bit similar to (although naturally not identical to) Simondon and Stiegler's coindividuation in that both regard emotional energy as an intermediary through which people can connect. But whereas Simondon and Stiegler's coindividuation is connection with others established via emotions or feelings that results in a two-way relationship of mutual assistance, love, and reciprocity, Levinas's ethics makes the other its first priority. It is in fact an unequal relationship in which the other supersedes the subject.

Levinas directly states that the other's strangeness is produced by the subject when the other calls into question the spontaneity of the same,[137] by which he means that, while the subject cannot easily grasp the strangeness of the other by the free exercise of consciousness and reason (the other is no longer an object of my knowledge), he or she must nonetheless take responsibility for the life of the other who is there in front of him or her (the other's *alterity* and *strangeness* link us).[138] This is the beginning of the true ethical experience, which is both an *ethical interruption* and a surprising transcendence.[139] How can this be an ethical interruption? Levinas, a phenomenologist, believes that the *primordial mode of the human existence* is *sensibility*[140] and *corporeality*[141] rather than reason and consciousness. As a result, contact with the corporeal other will often create an initial intuitive experience derived from the senses, and this precedes (or occurs faster than) it can be rationally calculated or controlled—to be face to face is rudimentary, affective, and sensual. This powerful ethical force transforms the disaffected and detached subject, who is always egocentric and situated in a position of transcendent knowledge, into an emotionally responsible subject. The entire experience, however, is involuntary and occurs while the subject is in a passive state, so it is an *interruption*.

In *Totality and Infinity*, Levinas dedicates many pages to phenomenological description of the Other-dominated ethical experience. He responds to the subject-prioritizing, Other-suppressing rationalist framework by inverting it, pointing out that when the subject encounters the other, not only is their relation not symmetrical, but the subject does not supersede the other; their relationship is in fact decidedly asymmetrical, with the other superseding the subject and even taking ownership of the subject's ethical relationship. In his later book *Otherwise than Being or Beyond Essence*, Levinas envisions the other as not just transcending the subject, but also as appearing phantom-like in front of that unaware individual and commanding the subject to be responsible for him or her: "The neighbor [the other] assigns me [the subject] before I designate him. This is a modality not of a knowing, but of an obsession, a shuddering of the human quite different from cognition"[142] and "the neighbor strikes me before striking me."[143] The other always flashes into existence with an ethical appeal, the command for the subject to take responsibility for the other being an infinite and imperative call.

Why can't the subject reject the other's imperative call? Here Levinas uses the *face of the other* to explain that the other's appeals are irresistible and subversive, making it impossible for the subject to reject them. Levinas points out that the face of the other is not only a physical face, but a *sensible appearance*[144] and an *epiphany*,[145] meaning that it is material and emotional:

> The face is not of the order of the seen, it is not an object, but it is he whose appearing preserves an exteriority which is also an appeal or an imperative given to your responsibility.[146]

The face of the other shows the other at his or her most naked and vulnerable, yet also reveals the other's most mysterious aspect:

> The disclosing of a face is nudity, non-form, abandon of self, ageing, dying, more naked than nudity.[147]

This unique, vulnerable, and suffering face of the other, like the hurt faces of the Old Testament's helpless foreigners, poor, and widows, disturbs the subject and makes him or her uneasy. Often the subject is moved by the pain in the face of the other before there has been time to decide what to do or how to respond to the other using theory or cognition. Levinas therefore points out that the face of the other is an *imperative face*. It says *no* to authority and also beseeches the subject with the message, "you shall not commit murder."[148] This results in the subject always feeling that he or she is not doing enough, has arrived too late, or is in fact being accused by the other so that the subject always feels that something more is owed.[149]

The suffering in the face of the other strikes a chord in the subject's sensible world, prompting the subject to invest in, suffer for, and even sacrifice for the other. Because the other usually appears quite suddenly, the subject is often forced to invest unhesitatingly (to sacrifice the self for justice?) without first calculating the cost, making the subject's ethical practice non-utilitarian and non-calculating. This is different from the rational subject, who reduces ethics to thought that is both utilitarian and calculated. Take firefighters as an example. They are unable to predict which victims they will encounter at the scene of a fire, but even if the cylinder on their back contains only enough oxygen for their own use, as soon as they see someone suffering from oxygen deficiency and calling for help, they are moved by the suffering face of the other and will save that person without regard for their own safety, even if they die as a result. Levinas's emotional subject does not therefore rely on the subject's own will and willingness to carry out justice. (He then takes this reasoning a step further, stating that any action taken after calculating the cost is not truly ethical.) Because the subject is always inclined to be egocentric, an extrinsic force (the suffering of the other) must *compel* the subject to take responsibility for the other.

The relationship of subject and other is no longer a hierarchical relationship of superior and inferior (the superior subject controlling the inferior other), but an ethical relationship in which the roles are reversed. That is, the superior-inferior relationship has been transformed from an intellectual, hierarchical relationship into an ethical relationship where the other is no longer the subject's intellectual inferior, but an object of responsibility that determines the meaning of the subject's existence. In *Otherwise than Being or Beyond Essence*, Levinas uses the analogy of a hostage, as if the subject has been kidnapped by and lost his freedom to the other's highly subversive abilities. Levinas calls this state of the other who is dependent on the subject a *proximity* relationship, an irreducible primordial relationship between the subject and the other. The unique, vulnerable, and suffering face of the other subverts Western philosophy's assumption of an *egoist subject* who prioritizes rationality, self-interest, and self-fulfilment—a disinterested subject.

Once the other has transformed the subject's life, the subject no longer controls the other but will suffer with and may even undergo trauma at his or her hands. This turns the subject into a suffering, weak, passive, and decentred *weak subject*, or in Critchley's terms, a *traumatic subject*.[150] The subject and the other must experience shared suffering, which is *gratuitous*, the subject standing by the other's side and listening sympathetically for the other's benefit. But when the subject shares the other's suffering, the ego's defences are removed and the subject's vulnerabilities exposed to the face of the other. The subject is linked with and submits to the life of the other, and in experiencing the other's trauma as his or her own becomes a genuinely ethical subject: "To be oneself, otherwise than being, to be dis-interested, is to bear the wretchedness and bankruptcy of the other";[151] "the subjectivity of subjection of the self is the suffering of suffering, the ultimate offering oneself. Subjectivity is vulnerability, is sensibility."[152]

The more the subject feels the pain of the other, the greater the subject's debt to the other becomes, and he or she will quite naturally want to respond to the other's imperative call by renouncing an egocentric life of pleasure. But Critchley argues that the subject is constantly *divided* by the other's *traumatic heteronomous demands*; he or she lives in a continual state of wanting to respond to the other's ethical call but is *split* between the self and the other's demands, which can never be fully met.[153] This, according to Levinas, is why the ethical subject's uniqueness is no longer based on *moral achievement*—that is, the regular, complacent examination of the self's goodness—

but is instead based on the subject's *fault*, inadequacy, and vulnerability. Influenced by the other, the subject's *lack* no longer derives from the self's unsatisfied desires, but from never being able to satisfy the ethical demand of the other.

The Emotional Politics Generated by Suffering

Within all the various right- and left-wing, anti- and pro-establishment political movements and politicking, the appropriation of *emotion* often tends towards one of two extremes. One of these is to unconditionally affirm the importance of all emotions (such as pleasure and anger) to politics and political mobilization without any recognition that emotional ethics has value. As long as it helps to stir up the public, for example, even hate-based violence is permissible, and hate will sometimes even be used to manufacture an *evil other* that is the rationalization for violence. As Slavoj Žižek has pointed out, even if most of the Nazi claims about the Jews were true—they exploit Germans; they seduce German girls—which they were not, of course, their anti-Semitism would still be (and was) pathological, since it represses the true reason why the Nazis *needed* anti-Semitism in order to sustain their ideological position: the Nazis believed their society to be a harmonious and cooperative organic whole, so they required a foreign aggressor in order to acknowledge differences and antagonisms within that whole.[154] In other words, violent politics always needs a scapegoat in order to foment hatred. Without this scapegoat, the entire political movement would collapse.

But the other extreme is to completely deny the importance of emotion in politics. This requires resorting to a modern form of entirely rational communication politics that promotes political action based solely on logical argument, balanced priorities, and effectiveness. This extreme, however, ignores that to uphold justice, a person must sometimes act out of responsibility and obligation, even if your actions do not have any immediate result or will negatively impact your personal interests. This obligation is especially true of actions that support the victimized other (such as events where the Tiananmen Square victims of June 4 are mourned). This is not to say that rational discussion is unimportant, but to point out that rationally driven social action may become overly calculated, utilitarian, and self-protective despite having transformed political action into a responsible ethical politics or ethical experience. Levinas's ethics of the other gives priority to the subject's sensible ethical experience, placing it ahead of all theory, rationality, and doctrine. On the one hand, this type of ethics affirms the importance of emotions in forming the subject's ethical experience, meaning that it is physical, sensible experience that pushes the subject to take responsibility for the other rather than a government body, the state, laws, or rational calculation doing so; on the other hand, it does not unconditionally affirm all emotions. On the contrary, it magnifies the feelings of pain, trauma, and even indebtedness stemming from the other, as well as the ethical qualities of these, thereby promoting an emotional politics based not on hatred but love (libido).

This type of responsibility- and compassion-driven politics based on the other's suffering and lack is much more desirable than social participation driven by hate or anger. I do not deny the importance of the latter two emotions, especially their positive value in expressing injustice. If a protest movement is to be carried out long term, however, both these emotions must gradually be transformed into powerful compassion. Otherwise, the end result may be violent politics. Isn't this the problem with much of today's right-wing populist politics?

Critchley places immense value on the ethical experience of sharing the other's suffering. This is because without it, ethical introspection becomes nothing more than an empty understanding of assorted ethical theories (such as discussions about what deontology and utilitarianism are),[155] while the ethical motivation that creates the ethical subject — an emotional experience of shared suffering with the other — is ignored.

By emphasizing the subject's freedom and need to endure the infinite demand of the other's face, this Other-oriented politics is able to limit the subject's *saviour/hero complex*, so that the subject who participates in it no longer prioritizes the will and authority of the *I*. (In some cases, some social activists eventually constitute another hegemony, ending up "on top of the heap".) It can prevent the subject from constantly aggrandizing his or her own supposed importance and greatness, and ultimately permits humble connection and cooperation with a greater number of people. The most dangerous part of the saviour/hero complex is that it results in individuals who think they can control everything and see themselves as the protagonist, central to the entire political movement. When the movement suffers setbacks, the participants who think of themselves this way are more likely to feel hopeless and become cynical. In contrast, if the goal is to meet the other's needs rather than the needs of the self, the subject may have a greater ability to weather temporary setbacks and quietly await the next opportunity. This is even more a question of how an individual's *commitment* is oriented.[156] Is your political participation a commitment to personal interests or to the interests of the other? If you have no understanding of the ethical motivations underlying political reform, you may become involved in political movements that emphasize power and self-interest and end up the very thing you wished to overthrow. Ultimately, therefore, Levinas's ethics of the other is not dealing with the problem of the other but rather the problem of *moral selfhood* or the ethical subject.[157] Finally, the political orientation that comes out of this ethics of the other emphasizes humility — it is flexible, not rigid; decentring, not controlling; love only, not rationality only; selfless, not self-aggrandizing. It makes an active subject take risks in an unknowable world and loves with wisdom all those who are suffering in this world.

It should also not be forgotten, as pointed out at the beginning of this chapter, that in Levinas's ethical politics of the other, the subject is an *anarchic subject* responsible only for the other and uninterested in personal benefit. This subject is not loyal to any government body, usually insists on dissent, and constantly confronts and criticizes oppressive regimes.[158] Anarchism stresses that political action and social governance don't require any political agent in the form of a government, political party, or state, much less that an individual give allegiance or devotion to any of these. Levinas considers anarchism's opposition to all sovereignty of the state to be a constant and thorough *disturbance* of it, one that persistently rejects and challenges the state as a whole by refusing to acknowledge it.[159] I consider *enemy/friend logic* and *populism* to now too often dominate political and social action given the overbearing state nationalism and narrowly-defined regionalism of current times. Perhaps the anarchic subject, anti-statist and responsible only for the other due to the sympathy the other evokes, can prevent the subject from falling into the traps of political patriotism and narrowminded nationalist politics.

I of course do not mean that establishing any sort of social order or system should be rejected, but that not all social orders and systems (including so-called democratic systems) regard establishing an ideal social system as the ultimate goal of political resistance (although this does not mean they fail to strive for a just and humane system); they also forget the priority and ultimacy of the other in all social action. As long as there is a suffering other who constantly reappears to accuse the subject for not taking responsibility, we have the basis of Levinas's argument for *recurrence of persecution*.[160] Because the subject can never take away the other's suffering and will be disappointed and suffer as a result of the other's constant disturbances, it's possible for ethical motivation to be sustained. This is a sobering *politics of disappointment*, a realpolitik that has no illusions about ideology, state, system, or political party. It is an entirely anarchist politics. This type of politics not only has the potential to transform the disaffected subject into an emotional subject, but also to establish a universalist politics of the other.

Take, for example, events that commemorate massacre in Myanmar. Such events do not necessarily spring out of a nationalist perspective, but from a wish to remember the other's suffering. Massacre in Myanmar is in fact a contest between forgetting and remembering. To preserve a memory is an ethical manifestation of the struggle against power and violence. This is because violent regimes always hope to erase the history of the oppressed or distort their memories of violent treatment. Levinas believes that the other brings *synchronicity* and *diachronicity* when he or she appears in the subject's life, and that although a person may be dead and so no longer have corporeal form, that individual can nonetheless come and go in the subject's life at any time, transcending time and space to manifest and hold the subject accountable. From this it is clear that the subject's silent meditation to mourn the other is ethical; it subverts our egocentric indulgence in a life of pleasure and creates the historical responsibility that permits the subject to shoulder this weight. It even has the potential to reverse history. For Levinas, therefore, there is no linear history—recalling the suffering faces of the other can alter the present and the future. Perhaps this is also the greater significance of mourning various massacres in the world.

Byung-Chul Han makes another observation that is not easily ignored: today's society, which encourages positivity and tends toward sameness, is also a homogeneous society from which the other, subjective negativity (e.g., pain and challenges), and difference have disappeared. Even digital media erases any distance between the self and the other before it proceeds to eliminate the other entirely.[161] On the one hand, the subject cares only about him- or herself, investing excess libidinal energy solely in the ego and so becoming a pathological narcissist.[162] Through self-improvement/actualization, subjects exploit themselves[163] in order to excel in an emotional capitalist society. On the other hand, the subject is constantly fleeing from and fighting the impact of the other on the ego, which withers the spirit and turns him or her into an *immune subject* undisturbed by the other. This is why Han states that it will be increasingly difficult for us to hear what Levinas described as the call of the other,[164] and also why it will also be increasingly difficult to be awakened by the enigma that is the other.[165]

I don't entirely agree with Han's argument, however. Actually, the problem we have today is not whether the other has disappeared. The other invariably exists and will never give the subject a means of escape. Rather, the crucial point is to ask: how do we explain having turned a blind eye to the other's existence? How have we made all sorts of excuses to rationalize the plight of the suffering other, and to rationalize our indifference? (As, for example, when we refuse to accept refugees because we are worried that they will have difficulty assimilating in another country and so will create more problems.) As for why we have turned a blind eye to the other, what kind of social environment causes this? I think neither Han's achievement society nor homogenizing society provides a full and sufficient explanation, although he has indeed been able to point out some of the problems stemming from today's narcissistic culture. I think, however, that the problem of the other's "disappearance" is not unrelated to today's authoritarian capitalism, which is constantly isolating or eliminating the suffering other. I will discuss this topic further in the next chapter.

Chapter 4

From the Ethical Subject to the Mourning Subject: Judith Butler on the Ethics of Mourning and Precarious Life

Our shared exposure to precarity is but one ground of our potential equality and our reciprocal obligations to produce together conditions of liveable life.

—Judith Butler

The previous chapter, which discussed Emmanuel Levinas's view that the suffering face of the other can arouse pity in a disaffected subject and transform him or her into an affective subject, helped to address Stiegler's concerns about an indifferent subject. But, while Byung-Chul Han has pointed out how today's tendency toward a homogenized achievement society and the *disappearance of the other* has resulted in narcissistic subjects difficult to emotionally affect, I consider this disappearance a problem that is in fact related to authoritarian capitalism having sequestered and eliminated the suffering other. In the current neoliberal environment of comprehensive marketization, our society has gradually marginalized disadvantaged groups with low productivity and low spending power and made them vulnerable. It has moved them to remote areas (China's domestic clean-up of its *low-end population*, for example, or Hong Kong's urban renewal that has relocated society's lowest rungs to rural areas) or reduced them to numbers (the government excels at turning the poor into data) in order to downplay or eliminate the other's very real life stories and problems. This is done in an attempt to deal with problems more quickly, such as getting rid of hawkers, driving out helpless refugees, etc.

Capitalism's Precarious Lives

As the sociologist Zygmunt Bauman has noted, our world has become a liquid society teeming with multicultural collisions and extraordinarily rapid population flow. This flow of people moving in and out contains innumerable others and strangers, such as refugees, people with no home or country, immigrants... The existence of such people naturally poses a threat and is a burden to the state. They are unwelcome because their cultures and customary lifestyles often deviate from the values of the state (including religion, neoliberalism, the national community culture, etc.), and even perhaps because they pose a threat to the local social order. Entire groups of such others are often treated as *waste* or even killed by the state. Bauman uses the term *wasted lives* to refer to this class of *wasted humans*.[166]

Bauman, who was influenced by the German legal philosopher Carl Schmitt's view of politics as a distinction between friend and enemy and also his assertion that sovereignty is determined by the sovereign, points out that Schmitt lived during the early twentieth century, an era in which multiple religions and cultures were in mutually antagonistic competition. For Schmitt, it followed that Germany had to rise above and overcome this clash of multiple values. Consensus was not established through discussion and dialogue between countries, but the need for each country to establish friend-enemy relations with other nations—to destroy their enemies by *association* and *dissociation* with other countries, or perhaps even by *association-through-dissociation*.[167] Bauman points out that this kind of friend-enemy thinking still exists in today's liquid society, especially when the neoliberal economics of *big market, small government* fails to preserve national security. Take, for example, the threat of terrorism against the United States, which made it necessary for the state to increase its own national or sovereign power to protect the country and its democratic system, of which it has always been so proud. Thus, on the one hand, a sovereign state will mass produce the enemies it wants eliminated (simultaneously creating many refugees, as when Buddhist Burmese wished to get rid of the Rohingya Muslims), while on the other hand, the sovereign power arbitrarily takes advantage of national laws, asserting it is under threat from an enemy and as a result must enter an urgent state of exception. Under the guise of the "sanctity" of law, the state then arbitrarily carries out violence against the other and even its own citizens, invading other countries and expelling refugees, for example, or imprisoning/killing those who leak national secrets, all in the name of anti-terrorism.

In turn, Isabell Lorey points out that *precarious life* in today's capitalism includes labourers and short-term contract workers (including outsourced workers) from various industries and labour niches who are exploited, isolated, and controlled by the system. Their work is not only dangerous (they work in extremely dangerous industries) but offers no safeguards (medical care, housing). Because no one is fighting for their rights, just to live places them in a precarious state.[168] This is especially true in a neoliberal society—in Hong Kong, for example, the government is very cautious about any welfare policies that aid disadvantaged groups, afraid of encouraging their self-reliance, as has happened in the past. An emphasis on self-improvement in addition to commodifying the body, emotions, and labour add up to a neoliberal philosophy that doesn't require any government involvement. Yet this sort of philosophy not only fails to help disadvantaged groups escape from their precarious lives, it actually increases their precarity. The government doesn't pretend to ignore the precariousness of a life in which "no work, no income" might occur at any time (despite its role in creating this situation); instead, it attempts to *normalize the precarization.* (I would like to make it clear that this is a normal state of affairs, not at all unique to Hong Kong.) The government then threatens residents into continuous self-improvement to ensure that they become *antiviral subjects* (using fear as a means of managing citizens), and doing their utmost to do nothing, or at least nothing of their own accord, to improve the welfare system and assist them. This is why Han asserts there is merely self-exploitation rather than exploitation by the system in today's neoliberal society (as discussed in the previous chapter). His observation is not wholly correct, however. At best, we can only say the techniques of exploitation the system employs have improved to the point that it no longer needs to actively manage citizens. It has instead taught the citizens to manage their own precarity and thus increase the speed at which the system can operate.[169]

American cultural theorist Judith Butler also adds to the discussion, stating that *precarity* does not indicate an individual's weak nature or character but signifies that we become vulnerable when our physical well-being is tied to fragile life conditions. (This is somewhat similar to German sociologist Ulrich Beck's globalized *risk society*.) These conditions are an interlocking network of politics, economics, and culture that may collapse at any time. And should any part of this network in fact collapse (such as during a period of financial turmoil, a war, or an epidemic, for example), sustaining the physical body will prove difficult. Such vulnerable lives may even be arbitrarily snuffed out by an authority that does not value them. To think critically about the world through a common experience of life's precariousness is not to rationalize the precarity, but to think about how life may be sustained and to seek ways of creating, strengthening, and revitalizing the various conditions that make life possible (such as political and economic systems).[170] Butler uses precarity to illustrate a tragic *dispossession* of the other: individuals who are violently seized by the sovereign or the system and forcibly stripped of their personal possessions (family, land, citizenship).[171] For those in situations of precarity, their self-identity is pulled up by the roots and destroyed while they remain helpless under the invader's thumb. Under racial segregation policies, for example, the activities of black people were restricted to certain places specified by those in power. Essentially, such measures placed black people in the precarity of *non-being*.[172]

Unfortunately, capitalist society is constantly creating precarity, continually tidying away in remote locations society's lowest rungs, those with *low antiviral power* who possess neither production nor consumer power. This is done firstly to keep us from seeing them, and secondly to make urban spaces into consumer spaces that permit only pleasure and discourage any expression of grief. Often, the reason many people feel that life holds no hope and choose to take their own lives is due to feeling neglected or rejected. I remember the public housing I lived in when I was young. Front doors were frequently left open and neighbours knew each other well. In those days, there was still space for "setting down your burdens", which permitted groups of women who looked after the home and took care of various household chores to share each other's joys and sorrows. Today, however, this kind of neighbourly emotional living space is difficult to come by, and this has eliminated many opportunities for the other to appear in our lives.

You might of course ask, doesn't social media put us in contact with any number of suffering others on a daily basis? Considering that social media prevails by speed,[173] even if we are exposed to a wide assortment of the suffering other each day, that much exposure can leave us numb to and even cause us to deliberately avoid seeing them. For Levinas, the suffering face of the other is irreproducible, its suffering perceivable only through our felt emotions (although we are never able to grasp it in its entirety; see the previous chapter). This is not to say that the suffering face is completely immaterial and therefore unseeable, but that seeing and images are not enough to convey the weight of the suffering other, let alone any ethical weight.

Consider, too, that social media is dominated by visuals and images that require us only to *look* and look quickly at that. It doesn't permit a gradual reaction to the other's suffering. Still more, it turns the other's body into a *stereotype* or *generic image*, so that even emotional and physical injury are *nullified* or *eliminated*.

As Butler says, the media will even go to the extent of using these *stereotyped images* to justify war and rationalize indiscriminate violence. They turn an image of Osama bin Laden into the face of terror, for example, or portray Saddam Hussein as the actual face of tyranny.[174] Alternatively, the media might give widespread coverage to the faces of Islamic women who have stripped off their burkas after their liberation by the U.S. military, thereby whitewashing the violence that has trampled another political regime.[175] But it is not true, as Butler says, that the other has been *dehumanized*,[176] or as the left wing likes to say, that the other has been *objectified*. Despite their frequent appearances as stereotyped images in the news, we still believe these are human beings. They are already so familiar to us, however, that we think we know all about them, and so it becomes quite natural for us to no longer care about them or even to hear the grief or suffering in their voices.[177] In other words, because they are insufficiently *alien* to us, that is, they don't fully constitute what Levinas calls *alterity*, we are less easily moved, less emotionally involved, less caring. Because these faces have been turned into images with no moral weight and so do not show us the human suffering Levinas describes, we may deduce that it is because these faces have been turned into images that the real ones have become inaccessible to us.

Collective Mourning as Public and Ethical Performance

Butler also points out that "one would need to hear the face [of the suffering other] as it speaks in something other than language to know the precariousness of life that is at stake."[178]

This is why I think we need more public spaces in which we grieve *with* and *for* the suffering other, a type of space that is material and emotional and in which physical togetherness, words, music, and visualizing the other allow everyone to mourn and show care for each other. This would allow not only the weak call of the other to be heard and attended to, but also permit feelings of precarity to be addressed. It would even make possible the public rather than private stimulation of those emotions that encourage social justice. Butler believes that, far from being negative or a show of weakness, affirming life's precariousness is extraordinarily positive, and that doing so can become the ethical motivation for social criticism or assuming responsibility for the other. On this point, Butler agrees with Levinas. Butler, however, proposes that we should make visible this abstract and previously invisible emotional force, suggesting that we establish a public emotional space in which we express *solidarity* with the alien other, thus making such expressions into reflections on society's unjust performance of public ethics and transforming them into possibilities for political mobilization.

Butler believes that collective mourning for the suffering other (refugees, labourers, the politically persecuted, sexual minorities...) can be a display of public emotion. She also points out that mourning for lost lives can cause unconscious or unexpected personal transformation and change. While mourning, the many things we can't know are often more likely to rise to the surface than what we can. As Freud states, when a person loses something, that person often does not know what has actually been lost. *Loss* is therefore at times like a riddle we struggle to solve but also another opportunity for self-exploration.[179] By the same token, mourning those we have lost allows us to reconsider what meaning an *I* attributes to the other, and especially how the *I* has been defined by the other in the past and what ties exist to bind them together. The *I* is awoken from a *self*-absorbed world, which as Stiegler suggests (and was also discussed in the previous chapter) assists in re-establishing a sense of *we*. It also allows us to rediscover a relationship with an other Levinas refers to as the *neighbour*, a relationship that the other will typically take over. Butler asserts that when an individual feels the other's pain, it amounts to an emotional disruption that forces the individual out of his or her disaffected state into an affective one:

> One does not always stay intact. One may want to, or manage to for a while, but despite one's best efforts, one is undone, in the face of the other, by the touch, by the scent, by the feel, by the prospect of the touch, by the memory of the feel.[180]

Naturally, my remembering and mourning the other does not bring the dead back to life, but even from the perspective of utilitarianism or political realism, mourning the other whom those in power have had killed or imprisoned (e.g., political prisoners and dissidents) can be a threat to power. (The Czech writer Milan Kundera once said: "The struggle of man against power is the struggle of memory against forgetting. *Because power often wants to erase the people's memory.*") But even if the other is not there with the subject or is dead, his or her suffering face can still transcend time and space to be "resurrected" in the subject's consciousness with the aid of the subject's attention, memory, and silent contemplation. The residue that the other leaves on the subject, which Levinas refers to as a *trace*, has both horizontal synchronicity and vertical diachronicity and can introduce a number of new thoughts for the subject. For example, what is a liveable life? What is an unliveable life? Why can I live happily but the other cannot? How have I been able to avoid misfortune, but they have not? (This is what the ancient Greek philosophers called *moral luck*.[181]) Why is the violence of some regimes so extreme? And what can I do?

As Stiegler points out, human memory has in large measure been handed over to the epiphylogenetic memory of electronic media in today's digital technology society. When the subject spontaneously engages in collective mourning for the other, memory combines libidinal and emotional energies (worry, unease, anger, or sadness). Of these latter energies, mourning may more effectively internalize or transfer libidinal energy into the emotional motivation to promote justice. This seems much like what Stiegler has said about the practice of attention, except that in this case, our focus shifts from an object to the other. Although mourning carried out in public spaces doesn't allow us to *see* the other, the gatherings in which we collectively remember can nonetheless create an affective space that morally inspires all of society. For this reason, even subjects not present at the gathering can have a deeper understanding of the suffering other's circumstances and be willing to take part in a collective stand. This is undoubtedly far better than one-dimensional information about the other obtained from the daily social media race.

Butler therefore believes that when we confront an unjust society, our public support, protest, and collective grief on behalf of the weak other constitutes a form of rebellion in which we courageously make ourselves vulnerable in order to resist or defy power, and that this is even more true when we do so in public spaces symbolic of power and authority. (For instance the Umbrella Movement in Hong Kong operated according to this logic.) For Butler, the courage required to take to the streets and resist by physically occupying a space is necessarily preceded by the courage and willingness to open our minds to the other and history. Furthermore, this openness is what constitutes *vulnerability*. In fact, for Butler, vulnerability does not have a negative meaning, nor is it a kind of *injurability*;[182] rather, vulnerability is to *come up against the outside world* as a performed modality of life and emotions,[183] it is to physically/

emotionally open ourselves to the unknown other and the world,[184] thereby initiating the process of exploring an unknown environment. (This is of course also the subject of Levinas's later research in *Otherwise than Being or Beyond Essence*, but Butler takes it further, transforming it into the ethical practice of social movements.) With this in mind, Butler's *vulnerability* is an ethical attitude or orientation, an expression of courage, commitment, and responsibility, but most of all an affective response, which for me makes it the foundation of an ethics of emotional politics.

Of course, traditional Western philosophy contains numerous discussions about human vulnerability, but it seldom affirms life's precariousness. The Stoics considered our human dignity so firm a core that it was effectively impervious to whatever the world might throw at us.[185] Nietzsche, despite seeing life as a tragedy, felt that this was all the more reason for a person to exert the will to power in daily life that would make him or her a superman, thus conquering and defying life's tragic nature. A superman could never be vulnerable, because the vulnerable are dominated by others and lack freedom; and to depend on someone else's pity was even more so to express a cowardly slave morality. Butler reminds us that vulnerability has long been equated with women and so has frequently been disregarded as a motivating force for ethical and political reform. (Which perhaps has something to do with men having typically initiated such reforms.)[186]

Accordingly, when everyone is in a public space marching, standing, observing a moment of silence, or singing on behalf of the suffering other, or when they call for protest against violent regimes, this is neither *routine ceremony* nor dispensable ritual but an expression of courage. They are taking a risk (of possible arrest or being placed under surveillance), which may result in their being suppressed alongside the other. It is also vulnerability politics put into practice, which includes bodily vulnerability and all the associated emotions, intonations, tears, or gestures that such vulnerability triggers and that may be equally interpreted as having to do with such abstract symbols as rights, equality, and freedom.

Using the example of Plato's prohibition against poets, Butler has also conjectured that those in power might wish to keep the citizens of a polis from witnessing too much tragedy, from crying for and mourning lost lives, or even from feeling the anger at life's injustices that ultimately causes collective mourning to evolve into a public gathering which threatens political authority and order.[187] The *bodily performance* of vulnerability that occurs during collective mourning is thus dangerous to political power, which means that totalitarian governments must always prevent or prohibit such seemingly harmless and peaceful public mourning (not to mention more "radical" demonstrations). What they oppose and suppress is not only the ceremony itself, but the "dangerous" emotions that mourning produces, for even though the body is vulnerable, it can also demonstrate the desire for justice.[188] This is why what Butler calls *political affects* are more likely to be generated during a crisis. These affects construct an emotional and physical space inclusive of everyone, which allows vulnerable sufferers to feel supported, recognized, and no longer alone. It also allows them to find an emotional community in which there is both *you and I* and which reminds its members that a liveable life must be a *grievable life*.[189] She points out that this is a bit like being in a war—my own life remains intact, but when I discover that the other's life has been destroyed, a part of my life is too.

Because the hedonic consumer subject of today's emotional consumerist society, which we could also call a competitive-speed prioritizing society, understands only the production and pursuit of speed and pleasure, this kind of slow, collective mourning practised as public emotion might well have no immediate effect. (Butler reminds us, however, that while feeling another's pain is a slow process, it can help us to identify with the suffering itself.[190]) Yet despite critiques of public mourning as overly emotional and meaningless, it can provide an alternative vision of political participation and lifestyle. More importantly, collective mourning in a caring community allows solitary individuals to form a heterogeneous emotional community full of complementary libidinal energies. Over time, this abundance of emotion can motivate a new round of reforms and open up new possibilities.[191] (To a certain extent, the 2019 anti-extradition movement in Hong Kong resulted from the reaccumulated and transformed energy of the 2014 Umbrella Movement. This process took just five years, which can be considered quite fast.) Butler therefore asserts that both collective mourning and protest, which are a bodily performance of rebellion that says "no" to the oppressor—and which could even be called a *turbulent performative occasion*[192]—can reclaim the dignity of a class of people once regarded as *naked lives* and thus satisfy the necessary conditions for establishing a democratic society. This point demonstrates that while Butler sees precariousness (an insecure living situation) as problematic, she also sees a positive side: it transforms suffering and injury into the sort of critique that motivates society.

Combining Emotional and Ethical Public Spaces

In addition to social movements serving as other-inclusive emotional spaces, we can also admit the other into the spaces we use on a daily basis, such as restaurants, markets, churches, or volunteer organizations, turning these consumer-labour spaces into emotional spaces used to rescue the other. For the German social philosopher Jürgen Habermas, the public sphere was a space for rational communication. His views influenced conventional thought so that discussions about the public sphere gradually came to regard the ideal public space as one that allows citizens to avoid *systematically distorted communication* and creates *ideal speech situations* by serving as a discussion space in which differing opinions can be freely expressed. But to describe the public sphere solely in these terms overlooks that it can also be a public emotional space in which an entire range of emotions may be expressed instead of suppressed. (In modern culture, emotions and the body have long been classified as private "things" not to be shown in public.) This would mean permitting certain "negative" emotions to be expressed, or even a space that welcomes, cares for, and protects those living precarious lives. The latter situation occurred in October 2018, when a Dutch church in The Hague protected a family of Armenian refugees. By welcoming the Tamrazyan family into the church and holding a worship service there for 50 consecutive days, 24 hours a day, Bethel Church was able to stop police from entering to arrest and deport the family. Offering the family "sanctuary" with this around-the-clock worship service was made possible by Dutch law, which prohibits police from entering religious sites during worship services. After a marathon of 96 days and more than 2,300 hours of prayer, the Dutch parliament finally agreed to apply the Children's Pardon, which allowed the entire family to remain in the country.

Of course, to admit the other is always full of tension. For a host to open his or her home and a country to admit the other is to risk a loss of sovereignty and a stable identity, among other hazards. This is why human beings always have doubts about admitting the other. After all, the *ethics of hospitality* always brings danger, impossibility, and subversion. But as Jacques Derrida says, we cannot escape this tension. If anything, we must inhabit it to remind the communities of close-minded nations and self-centred human beings to remain open. This is why Derrida reminds us not to throw out interpersonal alliances, unity, or community despite the necessity of deconstructing and rejecting all totalities. Rather than rejecting such things, his concern is simply that a homogeneous community does not kill the singularity of the other. As a result, he is preoccupied with whether there is space to accommodate and admit guests and strangers into the community. Of course, Derrida adds that complete acceptance of the other is at present difficult to implement fully and that this is something we can only look forward to in the future. But change begins with a single step, and it is only through taking risks that we can strive to realize this ethical responsibility.[193]

In any case, the Dutch church that took the risk of admitting the other was an awe-inspiring and significant instance of putting ethics into practice in today's precarious society. To assign emotional meaning to public spaces is not a rejection of rational dialogue's value. It is an indication that public space dominated by reason can no longer fully respond to our current emotional capitalist society and its crisis of precariousness. To understand public space as a space dominated by rationality is not only too intellectual and too middle-class, but it also places too much emphasis on a predominantly masculine temperament and disregards the lifestyles of ordinary people who prioritize caring and emotion in their daily lives. (A further example of this is the panic buying that occurred in 2020, when many Hong Kong residents rushed out to buy masks or toilet paper due to the outbreak of Covid-19. The intellectuals and government officials who accused them of overreacting ignored these residents' concerns and failed to see that their emotional reaction reflected their dissatisfaction with the government's inability to deal with the pandemic.) Civil society is likewise constituted from all-important emotional offerings of aid and rescue concealed in everyday urban spaces. (During the anti-extradition movement in Hong Kong, some restaurants supported the movement by providing supplies and even spiritual and emotional support to the protesters. And of course, nothing in this discussion is meant to imply that rational discussion belongs exclusively to intellectuals; often, ordinary citizens are in fact more reasonable and sensible about everyday life than intellectuals.)

Grief or Anger?

As someone might well point out, surely there is something besides grief that can give the other a voice? Can grief be the only way to affirm the other's precarity? Can't anger speak for the other? Indeed, anger too provides an important impetus for social reform, and its energy can later be transformed to generate numerous possibilities for the future. Anger is also frequently the main factor that launches mass social movements. But anger is short-lived and is therefore an emotion that cannot be relied on to create an inevitable or lasting motivation for pursuing justice. The queries above may be the questions that Martha C. Nussbaum, another female philosopher, attempts to answer in *Anger and Forgiveness*. She points out that sometimes anger is used to justify actions that cause a wrongdoer to suffer (such as the injured party humiliating and down-ranking the offender to vent his or her anger, retaliating against the other party in eye-for-an-eye style), with the idea that this person's suffering will improve his or her own situation.[194] But inflicting pain on the perpetrator without addressing one's own right or wrong behaviour or seeking to remedy the situation afterwards is simply an angry person overly intent on venting his or her resentment; retaliation does nothing to undo the injury already sustained, and at best will only serve as a deterrent against future wrongdoing. Nussbaum also disagrees with the idea that seeing wrongdoers get what's coming to them will bring people together, recognizing that anger simply increases violence and hatred.

The biggest problem with the two approaches outlined above—a focus on either retaliation or negatively affecting the perpetrator's relative status—is a single-minded wish for the perpetrator to suffer (physically or mentally) based on the mistaken belief that this will alleviate the injured party's pain. Neither approach helps the victim to recover from the injuries he or she has suffered. Even so, Nussbaum agrees victims should hold the wrongdoer accountable for the injuries they have suffered, and that it is only natural for society to assist them in this. But she also asserts that the law's punishment of wrongful acts should not be just a palliative or deterrent; its punishments must pave the way for a public accountability that prevents the same thing from happening again in future without eye-for-an-eye retaliation. Ultimately, Nussbaum believes that unconditional compassion can promote a just society better than anger can over the long run. She uses the example of Martin Luther King, Jr.: When he confronted the racial discrimination taking place in the United States of his time, he neither demonized white people nor encouraged black people to hate them, nor did he suggest retaliating against white people and causing them to suffer. Instead, he focused on a future in which blacks achieved equality and brotherhood with whites and called upon everyone to work together to create a just world in which blacks and whites could peacefully coexist.[195]

Of course, there's no need for us to reject the positive aspects of anger in promoting social justice. We just need to take care that *unconditional compassion* does not become an excuse to cover up injustices. (In cases of sexual harassment in the church, for example, the Christian teachings of compassion and forgiveness are often used by some to persuade female victims not to hold the other party accountable, although such people conveniently overlook that Christianity also talks about a love of justice.) I would even say that having the perpetrator experience the victim's suffering is not necessarily *revenge* as Nussbaum describes it, and that to do so permits the perpetrator to have a greater awareness of the harm that he or she has done to others. This then facilitates sincere repentance and more effectively promotes true institutional reform. The anti-anger and non-violent protest of Gandhi, Martin Luther King, and Mandela is certainly desirable, but without the cooperation of the angry masses, can a social movement actually be successful?

For this reason, whether anger is positive or negative often depends on the situation. Although anger may not be the motivating factor in an inevitable and long-term pursuit of justice, in the short-term, anger remains an indispensable part of mass movements, especially large-scale protest movements. That said, I nonetheless do believe that long-term justice based on compassion and love must be the driving force for building a civil society, and that Nussbaum's proposed *transition-anger* is a good idea, especially today, when right-wing populism is rampant and politicians are constantly using hatred to whip up the masses and thereby achieve a certain political goal.

Although both Butler and Nussbaum are interested in gender issues and emotional politics, they are scholars from different academic traditions. As a result, their emotional politics differ in significant ways. Butler, for example, places greater emphasis on demonstrating the body's emotional power in forms of street protest, while Nussbaum incorporates emotional elements into a legal framework. Several years ago, Nussbaum even wrote an article criticizing Butler's postmodernist, anti-essentialist position, asserting that the presuppositions in her work contain no essential thought, and that critique of sexual violence as unjust does not help to establish a foundation for ethics.[196] Nonetheless, both scholars recognize an anger that is not based on violence and the irrationality of fear. Emotional politics is instead based on compassion and grief, while to establish various emotional public spaces that bring people justice and hope even as they restore the dignity of the other is helpful, especially when fighting against precariousness, fear, or despair. I think both these two thinkers have fully demonstrated the greater possibilities for emotional politics. They have allowed us to have a deeper understanding and awareness of *ethical emotions* and *emotional ethics*, both of which are simply a response to the precarity and anxiety we find everywhere in capitalist society today.

Endnotes

1. Lauren Berlant, *Cruel Optimism* (Durham: Duke University Press, 2011), 53.
2. Sara Ahmed, *The Cultural Politics of Emotion* (New York: Routledge, 2004), 191.
3. Brian Massumi, trans., "Notes on the Translation and Acknowledgement" in *A Thousand Plateaus*, Gilles Deleuze and Felix Guattari (Minneapolis: University of Minnesota Press, 1987), xvi.
4. Michael Hardt, "Foreword: What Affects Are Good For" in *The Affective Turn: Theorizing the Social*, eds. Patricia Ticineto Clough and Jean Halley (Durham & London: Duke University Press, 2007), ix.
5. Ariel Ducey, "More than A Job: Meaning, Affect, and Training Health Care Workers" in *The Affective Turn: Theorizing the Social*, eds. Patricia Ticineto Clough and Jean Halley (Durham & London: Duke University Press, 2007), 191.
6. Eric Shouse, "Feeling, Emotion, Affect", *M/C Journal*, Volume 8, Issue 6 (December 2005): 1/3.
7. Eva Illouz, *Cold Intimacies: The Making of Emotional Capitalism* (Cambridge: Polity Press, 2007), 3.
8. Lawrence Grossberg (interviewed by Gregory J. Seigworth & Melissa Gregg), "Affect's Future: Rediscovering the Virtual in the Actual" in *The Affect Theory Reader*, eds. Melissa Gregg and Gregory J. Seigworth (Durham & London: Duke University Press, 2010), 309.
9. Brian Massumi, *Parables for the Virtual: Movement, Affect, Sensation* (Durham & London: Duke University Press, 2002), 45.
10. Byung-Chul Han, *Psychopolitics: Neoliberalism and New Technologies of Power* (London: Verso, 2017), 44-6.

11. Illouz, *Cold Intimacies*, 7.

12. Stjepan Meštrović, *Postemotional Society* (London: Sage, 1997), 25.

13. Ibid., 25.

14. Frank Weyher, "Re-Reading Sociology via the Emotions: Karl Marx's Theory of Human Nature and Estrangement", *Sociological Perspectives*, Volume 55, Number 2 (Summer 2012): 344.

15. Karl Marx and Friedrich Engels, *The Marx-Engels Reader*, ed. Robert C. Tucker (London: W.W. Norton & Company, 1978), 115.

16. Ibid., 74.

17. Of course, Erich Fromm and Wilhelm Reich also developed theories which synthesized the ideas of Marx and Freud, but because their discussions of libidinal economy fall short in comparison to those of Marcuse, Deleuze and Guattari, and Lyotard, they will not be included here.

18. Jean Laplanche and J.-B. Pontalis, *The Language of Psycho-Analysis* (New York: W.W. Norton & Company, 1973), 127-29.

19. Herbert Marcuse, *Eros and Civilization* (London: Sphere Books LTD, 1970), 169.

20. Bernard Stiegler, "A Rational Theory of Miracles: On Pharmacology and Transindividuation", *New Formations*, 77 (2012): 169.

21. Jouissance refers to a more subversive force that transforms subjectivity while pleasure refers to a conservative force that simply justifies the existing status of subjectivity. See Roland Barthes, *The Grain of the Voice: Interviews 1962-1980* (New York: Hill and Wang, 1985), 206.

22. Bernard Stiegler, "A Rational Theory of Miracles: On Pharmacology and Transindividuation", 169.

23. See chapter four of this book.

24. Gilles Deleuze and Felix Guattari, *Anti-Oedipus: Capitalism and Schizophrenia* (Minneapolis: University of Minnesota Press, 1982), 1.

25. Gilles Deleuze, *Negotiations, 1972-1990*, trans. Martin Joughin (New York: Columbia University Press, 1995), 180.

26. Maurizio Lazzarato, *Signs and Machines: Capitalism and the Production of Subjectivity* (South Pasadena: Semiotext(e), 2014), 25.

27. In *Nietzsche and Philosophy*, Deleuze points out that Nietzsche regarded the body as an organism composed of a multiplicity of forces. The body is engaged in a tug of war between these various forces, which may be chemical, biological, social, or political. It may thus be inferred that "being composed of a plurality of irreducible forces the body is a multiple phenomenon, its unity is that of a multiple phenomenon, a 'unity of domination.' In a body the superior or dominant forces are known as *active* and the inferior or dominated forces are known as *reactive*. Active and reactive are precisely the original qualities which express the relation of force within force." For Nietzsche, forces are therefore not all the same. He assigned great importance to a dominant force because it permits the subject's life to become powerful, with the result that the person becomes an "Overman" and not "the last man". The last man rejects suffering and seeks only a life of unchanging degeneracy. He or she either simply adapts to circumstances or is content to give in to the domination of the environment and thereby lose both autonomy and freedom. Lacking the courage to change the environment, this person rejects control over his or her will to power. Nietzsche therefore demanded that a person establish an interior "active plastic force" to transcend and overcome the reactive forces of the body, transforming them into the creative freedom of the will to power and regaining control

over the rest of the body. Establishing this force can also give people the courage to confront the challenges of life, especially in a life of tragic suffering. To take this a step further, much like an artist creates a work of art, the creation of one's own life overturns the laws that enslave and oppress a person and establishes a uniquely aesthetic life. Deleuze believes that Nietzsche at a fundamental level saw the body as a sage because "the body's active forces make it a self and define the self as superior and astonishing." In fighting against an oppressive world, a person must have the Overman's will of rebellious impulse. Further, the Overman's will to revolt does not stem from abstract consciousness but from the body's arousal. Nietzsche's understanding of the body's potential lets us see that to rely on rational thought alone is not enough for the subject to rebel against the world. Instead, it is a return to the body that stimulates its forces and brings about real change. The problem, however, is that the Overman must frequently overcome the last man, and can this then be considered domination by violence?

28. Jean-François Lyotard, *Libidinal Economy* (Bloomington and Indianapolis: Indiana University Press, 1993), 95.

29. Ibid., 111.

30. Bernard Stiegler, "A Rational Theory of Miracles: On Pharmacology and Transindividuation", 177.

31. Laplanche and Pontalis, *The Language of Psycho-Analysis*, 13.

32. It will have a detailed discussion in chapter two.

33. It will have a detailed discussion in chapter two.

34. In his 1976 "Society Must Be Defended" lectures at the Collège de France, the French philosopher Michel Foucault stated that from the end of the seventeenth to the eighteenth century, European nations attempted to regulate their citizens' lives, health, hygiene, birth rate

and other demographic factors, and that these attempts were an excuse to control the people's lives or *form of life* (e.g., birth control and lifestyle) through the use of various *techniques of regulation* and *techniques of discipline* that ensured their cooperation with national population policy developments. Foucault called this power to regulate/control lives biopower.

35. Byung-Chul Han, *Psychopolitics*, 45.
36. Ibid., 46.
37. Ibid., 40.
38. Ibid., 5-6.
39. Chip Conley, *Emotional Equations: Simple Truths for Creating Happiness + Success* (New York: Free Press, 2012), 6-7.
40. Byung-Chul Han, *Psychopolitics*, 47.
41. Jean Baudrillard, *For a Critique of the Political Economy of the Sign* (St. Louis, MO: Telos Press, 1981), 146-7.
42. "Eva Illouz: comment nos émotions sont devenues des marchandises", *L'OBS*, March 2019. https://bibliobs. nouvelobs.com/idees/20190201.OBS9480/eva-illouz-comment-nos-emotions-sont-devenues-des-marchandises. html
43. Byung-Chul Han, *Psychopolitics*, 46.
44. Illouz believes it is not just consumers affected by emotional consumer culture, but also *prosumers*, the combination of *producer* and *consumer*. Illouz refers specifically to some DIY consumer products that allow consumers to make their own products, which creates a feeling of *self-complacent intimacy* with such items.
45. Byung-Chul Han, *In the Swarm: Digital Prospects*, trans. Erik Butler (Cambridge, Massachusetts: MIT Press, 2017), 33-34.
46. Byung-Chul Han, *Psychopolitics*, 14.
47. Sigmund Freud, *On Sexuality: Three Essays on the Theory of Sexuality and other Works* (London: Penguin Books, 1977), 362-3.

48. Byung-Chul Han, *The Burnout Society*, trans. Erik Butler (Stanford: Stanford University Press, 2015), 38.

49. Byung-Chul Han, *In the Swarm: Digital Prospects*, trans. Erik Butler (Cambridge, Massachusetts: MIT Press, 2017), 53.

50. Ibid., 54.

51. See chapter three in this book.

52. Agamben's homo sacer was a part of Roman criminal law. Sacer originally referred to those things set apart from society, which included the sacred and the cursed, while homo sacer referred to those whose social, civil, and religious rights had been revoked by Roman society or those in power, making these people a group of bare lives outside the law and without any right to life. Homo sacer are "sacred" not because they are pure, but because they are unclean or cursed and so cannot be sacrificed to the gods. Agamben has extended this idea to today's society. During some states of exceptional emergency (such as a terrorist attack), those in power will often strip perceived enemies of their right to life, using the excuse of safeguarding their own sovereignty. In doing so, they take no moral or legal responsibility, just as it used to be for the homo sacer of ancient Rome. For details, see Agamben, *Homo Sacer: Sovereign Power and Bare Life* (Stanford: Stanford University Press, 1998).

53. Byung-Chul Han, *The Burnout Society*, trans. Erik Butler (Stanford: Stanford University Press, 2015), 49.

54. *Bullshit jobs* is a term used by the American anthropologist and anarchist David Graeber to refer to the many instances of pointless work in today's capitalist society (such as endless meetings and discussions) that are neither effective nor meaningful. Graeber, *Bullshit Jobs: A Theory* (New York: Simon & Schuster, 2018), 21-22.

55. Barbara Ehrenreich, *Bright-Sided: How Positive Thinking Is Undermining America* (New York: Metropolitan Books, 2009), 2.

56. Ibid., 5.

57. Ibid., 77.

58. Byung-Chul Han, *The Transparency Society* (Stanford, California: Stanford University Press, 2015), 5-6.

59. Ibid., 7-8.

60. Arlie Russell Hochschild, *The Managed Heart: Commercialization of Human Feeling* (Berkeley and Los Angeles, California: University of California Press, 2012), 7.

61. Ibid., 5.

62. Ibid., 57.

63. Ibid., 104-5.

64. Ibid., 48.

65. Yuk Hui, Stiegler's student, translated the concept of *proletarianization* into Chinese as *dehumanization*. Hui points out that in Stiegler's understanding, *property* is not what defines the proletariat. On the contrary, to become a proletariat is a reflection of lost skill, just as a farmer loses skills by selling his labour in a factory, where he is obliged to work according to a mechanical process. Hui therefore thought it made more sense to translate the term *proletarianization* as *dehumanization*.

66. Bernard Stiegler, *Uncontrollable Societies of Disaffected Individuals* (Cambridge: Polity Press, 2012), 3.

67. Bernard Stiegler, *For a New Critique of Political Economy* (Cambridge: Polity Press, 2010), 33.

68. Ibid., 30.

69. Laurent de Sutter, *Narcocapitalism* (Cambridge: Polity Press, 2018), 44.

70. Ibid., 48.

71. Byung-Chul Han, *The Agony of Eros* (Cambridge: MIT Press, 2017), 19.

72. Christopher Lash, *The Culture of Narcissism: American Life in an Age of Diminishing Expectations* (New York: Warner Books, 1980), 33.

73. Han, *The Agony of Eros*, 25-6.

74. Bernard Stiegler, *Uncontrollable Societies of Disaffected Individuals: Disbelief and Discredit, Volume 2* (Cambridge: Polity Press, 2013), 79.

75. Bernard Stiegler, *Symbolic Misery, Volume 1: The Hyperindustrial Epoch* (Cambridge: Polity Press, 2014), 13.

76. It is similar to a spiritual practice of contemplation that trains a subject to be attentive to his or her surrounding world.

77. Gilbert Simondon, "The Genesis of the Individual", in *Incorporations*, eds. Jonathan Crary & Sanford Kwinter (New York: Zone Books, 1992), 307.

78. Ibid., 304.

79. Pascal Chabot, *The Philosophy of Simondon: Between Technology and Individuation* (London: Bloomsbury, 2003), 98.

80. Ibid., 77.

81. Robert Hughes, "Bernard Stiegler, Philosophical Amateur, Or, Individuation from Eros to Philia", *Diacritics*, Volume 42, Number 1 (2014): 47.

82. Stiegler, *Uncontrollable Societies of Disaffected Individuals*, 5.

83. Ibid., 3.

84. Ibid., 93.

85. Bernard Stiegler, *The Lost Spirit of Capitalism* (Cambridge: Polity, 2014), 2.

86. Bernard Stiegler, *Uncontrollable Societies of Disaffected Individuals*, 104.

87. Pieter Lemmens, "'This System Does Not Produce Pleasure Anymore': An Interview with Bernard Stiegler", *Krisis*, Issue 1 (2011): 36-7.

88. Bernard Stiegler, *Uncontrollable Societies of Disaffected Individuals*, 82.

89. Another characteristic of emotional labour is that more tasks are emotionally outsourced. As Hochschild points

out in her book *The Outsourced Self: Intimate Life in Market Times*, more and more American households and families are outsourcing to foreign or professional help the emotional care tasks that they could once do or handle themselves, such as hiring a caregiver to care for their parents.

90. Bernard Stiegler, *Symbolic Misery, Volume 1*, 2.
91. Bernard Stiegler, *Uncontrollable Societies of Disaffected Individuals*, 8.
92. Bernard Stiegler, *Uncontrollable Societies of Disaffected Individuals*, 105.
93. Bernard Stiegler, *Symbolic Misery, Volume 1*, 1.
94. Ibid., 3.
95. Ibid., 5
96. Zhang Yibing, *A Reading of Stiegler's Technics and Time as Situating Theory* (Shanghai: Shanghai People's Press, 2018), 18-9.
97. Bernard Stiegler, *Symbolic Misery, Volume 1*, 10.
98. Pieter Lemmens, "'This System Does Not Produce Pleasure Anymore': An Interview with Bernard Stiegler", 35.
99. Bernard Stiegler, *Symbolic Misery, Volume 1*, 3.
100. During the Umbrella Movement in Hong Kong, the protestors used artworks to cultivate a kind of consciousness of "we-ness" in the occupied area.
101. Bernard Stiegler, *Symbolic Misery, Volume 1*, 2.
102. Bernard Stiegler, *What Makes Life Worth Living: On Pharmacology* (Cambridge: Polity Press, 2013), 63.
103. Ibid., 69.
104. Ibid., 2.
105. Bernard Stiegler, *Taking Care of Youth and the Generations* (Stanford, California: Stanford University Press, 2010), 66.
106. Ibid., 73.
107. Bernard Stiegler, *Taking Care of Youth and the Generations*, 65.

108. In 2016, Bernard Stiegler raised this point during a lecture at Nanjing University. See Zhang Yibing, *A Reading of Stiegler's Technics and Time as Situating Theory*, p. 98, footnote 3.

109. Bernard Stiegler, *Taking Care of Youth and the Generations*, 82, 84.

110. Bernard Stiegler, *What Makes Life Worth Living*, 81.

111. Ibid., 64.

112. Ibid., 87.

113. Bernard Stiegler, *Symbolic Misery, Volume 2: The Catastrophe of the Sensible* (Cambridge: Polity Press, 2015), 106-7.

114. Ibid., 22.

115. Bernard Stiegler, *Symbolic Misery, Volume 2*, 164.

116. Martin Crowley, "The Artist and the Amateur, from Misery to Invention" in *Stiegler and Technics*, eds. Christina Howells and Gerald Moore (Edinburgh: Edinburgh University Press, 2013), 128.

117. Bernard Stiegler, *Uncontrollable Societies of Disaffected Individuals*, 90.

118. The *Anthropocene Epoch* is a concept proposed in 2000 by Dutch atmospheric chemist Paul Crutzen. Over the past three centuries, human activities (in particular the industrial revolution) have brought about massive and drastic geological change. This rapid change, and even ecological destruction, of the global environment has radically altered the appearance of the Earth's strata, launching a whole new geological period. Stiegler proposed the *Neganthropocene* as a response that could remedy the economic and ecological problems the Anthropocene has brought by using technology to reform society and transform technology's previous toxicity (*poison*) into an antidote (*medicine*) for liberating the world. He also proposed an *economy of potlatch* to modify a capitalist economic model that emphasizes occupation and

expropriation, as well as to develop technology and the economy in the hope of halting further *proletarianization*. See Bernard Stiegler, *Nanjing Lectures (2016-2019)* (English translation, 2020), originally quoted from the Chinese translation (2016) in Zhang Yibing, *A Reading of Stiegler's Technics and Time as Situating Theory*, p. 321.

119. Roberto Esposito, *Immunitas: The Protection and Negation of Life* (Cambridge: Polity Press, 2011), 4-5.

120. See Giorgio Agamben, *State of Exception* (Chicago: University of Chicago Press, 2005), 3.

121. Michael Hardt and Antonio Negri, *Multitude: War and Democracy in the Age of Empire* (New York: Penguin Books, 2004), 351.

122. Ibid., 352.

123. Simon Critchley, *Infinitely Demanding: Ethics of Commitment, Politics of Resistance* (London: Verso, 2007), 132.

124. Ibid., 194.

125. Ibid., 120.

126. See the preface in this book.

127. Tamra Wright, Peter Hughes, and Alison Ainley, "The Paradox of Morality: An Interview with Emmanuel Levinas", in *The Provocation of Levinas: Rethinking the Other*, eds. Robert Bernasconi and David Wood (London: Routledge, 1988), 176.

128. Jill Robbins, ed., *Is it Righteous to Be?: Interviews with Emmanuel Levinas* (Stanford, California: Stanford University Press, 2001), 173.

129. Emmanuel Levinas, *Totality and Infinity: An Essay on Exteriority*, trans. Alphonso Lingis (Pittsburgh, Pennsylvania: Duquesne University Press, 2001), 44.

130. Emmanuel Levinas, *Otherwise than Being or Beyond Essence*, trans. Alphonso Lingis (Pittsburgh, Pennsylvania: Duquesne University Press, 2002), 162.

131. Robbins, *Is it Righteous to Be?*, 113.

132. Emmanuel Levinas, *Totality and Infinity*, 43.

133. Ibid., 46-7.

134. Ibid., 46.

135. Ibid., 46.

136. Emmanuel Levinas, *Difficult Freedom: Essays on Judaism*, trans. Seán Hand (Baltimore: Johns Hopkins University Press, 1997), 206-7.

137. Emmanuel Levinas, *Totality and Infinity*, 43.

138. Robbins, *Is it Righteous to Be?*, 48.

139. Ibid., 48.

140. Emmanuel Levinas, *Otherwise than Being or Beyond Essence*, 14-5.

141. Ibid., 77.

142. Emmanuel Levinas, *Otherwise than Being or Beyond Essence*, 87.

143. Ibid., 88.

144. Emmanuel Levinas, *Totality and Infinity*, 198.

145. Ibid., 199.

146. Jill Robbins, *Is it Righteous to Be?*, 48.

147. Emmanuel Levinas, *Otherwise than Being or Beyond Essence*, 88.

148. Emmanuel Levinas, *Totality and Infinity*, 199.

149. Emmanuel Levinas, *Otherwise than Being or Beyond Essence*, 87.

150. Simon Critchley, *Infinitely Demanding*, 61.

151. Emmanuel Levinas, *Otherwise than Being or Beyond Essence*, 117.

152. Ibid., 54.

153. Simon Critchley, *Infinitely Demanding*, 62-3.

154. "Slavoj Žižek: What our fear of refugees says about Europe", *The New Statesman*, 29/2/2016, https://www.newstatesman.com/politics/2016/02/slavoj-zizek-what-our-fear-of-refugees-says-about-europe

155. Simon Critchley, *Infinitely Demanding*, 9.

156. Another French philosopher, Badiou, has also discussed the importance of *fidelity* in political action, but he believes that our fidelity must be to some history-changing *event*. Only then will our long-term commitment to the political movement triggered by that event be ensured and make us political subjects who actively support it. But are all such historical events ethical? For example, what about terrorist attacks? I think this is a question that requires serious thought. For Critchley's brilliant analysis of this topic, see Simon Critchley, *Infinitely Demanding*, 48-9.

157. Simon Critchley, *Infinitely Demanding*, 62.

158. Ibid., 194.

159. Emmanuel Levinas, *Otherwise than Being or Beyond Essence*, 194.

160. Ibid., 111.

161. Byung-Chul Han, *The Expulsion of the Other* (Cambridge: Polity Press, 2018), 65.

162. Ibid., 21-2.

163. Ibid., 38.

164. Ibid., 64.

165. Ibid., 68.

166. Zygmunt Bauman, *Wasted Lives: Modernity and Its Outcasts* (Cambridge: Polity Press, 2004), 12.

167. Zygmunt Bauman, "Seeking in Modern Athens an Answer to the Ancient Jerusalem Question", *Theory, Culture & Society*, Volume 26(1)(2009): 83.

168. Isabell Lorey, *State of Insecurity: Government of the Precarious* (London: Verso, 2015), 8.

169. Ibid., 26-7.

170. Judith Butler, *Frames of War: When Is Life Grievable?* (London: Verso, 2016), 23.

171. Judith Butler and Athena Athanasiou, *Dispossession: The Performative in the Political* (Cambridge: Polity Press, 2013), 3.

172. Ibid., 19.
173. Paul Virilio, *Lost Dimension* (New York: Semiotext(e), 1991), 35.
174. Judith Butler, *Precarious Life: The Powers of Mourning and Violence* (London: Verso, 2004), 141.
175. Ibid., 142.
176. Ibid., 148.
177. Ibid., 143.
178. Ibid., 151.
179. Ibid., 21.
180. Ibid., 23-4.
181. Martha C. Nussbaum, *The Fragility of Goodness: Luck and Ethics in Greek Tragedy and Philosophy* (Cambridge: Cambridge University Press, 1986).
182. Judith Butler, *Frames of War*, 34.
183. Ibid., 34.
184. Judith Butler, *Notes Toward a Performative Theory of Assembly* (Cambridge, Massachusetts: Harvard University Press, 2015), 149.
185. Martha C. Nussbaum, *The New Religious Intolerance: Overcoming the Politics of Fear in an Anxious Age* (Cambridge, Massachusetts: Harvard University Press, 2012), 66.
186. Judith Butler, *Notes Toward a Performative Theory of Assembly*, 123.
187. Judith Butler, *Frames of War*, 39.
188. Judith Butler, *Precarious Life*, 20.
189. Ibid., 15.
190. Ibid., 30.
191. Judith Butler and Athena Athanasiou, *Dispossession*, 178.
192. Ibid., 179.
193. Jacques Derrida and Anne Dufourmantelle, *Of Hospitality*, trans. Rachel Bowlby (Stanford, CA: Stanford University Press, 2000), 147.

194. Martha C. Nussbaum, *Anger and Forgiveness: Resentment, Generosity, Justice* (New York: Oxford University Press, 2016), 16-40.

195. Martha C. Nussbaum, *Anger and Forgiveness*, 31.

196. Martha C. Nussbaum, "The Professor of Parody: The hip defeatism of Judith Butler", *The New Republic Online*, February 23, 1999. Posted November 2000, https://newrepublic.com/article/150687/professor-parody

IFF
BOOKS

ACADEMIC AND SPECIALIST

Iff Books publishes non-fiction. It aims to work with authors and titles that augment our understanding of the human condition, society and civilisation, and the world or universe in which we live. If you have enjoyed this book, why not tell other readers by posting a review on your preferred book site. Recent bestsellers from Iff Books are:

Why Materialism Is Baloney

How true skeptics know there is no death and fathom answers to life, the universe, and everything
Bernardo Kastrup
A hard-nosed, logical, and skeptic non-materialist metaphysics, according to which the body is in mind, not mind in the body.
Paperback: 978-1-78279-362-5 ebook: 978-1-78279-361-8

The Fall

Steve Taylor
The Fall discusses human achievement versus the issues of war, patriarchy and social inequality.
Paperback: 978-1-78535-804-3 ebook: 978-1-78535-805-0

Brief Peeks Beyond

Critical essays on metaphysics, neuroscience, free will, skepticism and culture
Bernardo Kastrup
An incisive, original, compelling alternative to current mainstream cultural views and assumptions.
Paperback: 978-1-78535-018-4 ebook: 978-1-78535-019-1

Framespotting
Changing how you look at things changes how you see them
Laurence & Alison Matthews
A punchy, upbeat guide to framespotting. Spot deceptions
and hidden assumptions; swap growth for growing up. See
and be free.
Paperback: 978-1-78279-689-3 ebook: 978-1-78279-822-4

Is There an Afterlife?
David Fontana
Is there an Afterlife? If so what is it like? How do Western
ideas of the afterlife compare with Eastern? David Fontana
presents the historical and contemporary evidence for
survival of physical death.
Paperback: 978-1-90381-690-5

Nothing Matters
a book about nothing
Ronald Green
Thinking about Nothing opens the world to everything by
illuminating new angles to old problems and stimulating new
ways of thinking.
Paperback: 978-1-84694-707-0 ebook: 978-1-78099-016-3

Panpsychism
The Philosophy of the Sensuous Cosmos
Peter Ells
Are free will and mind chimeras? This book, anti-materialistic
but respecting science, answers: No! Mind is foundational to
all existence.
Paperback: 978-1-84694-505-2 ebook: 978-1-78099-018-7

Punk Science
Inside the Mind of God
Manjir Samanta-Laughton
Many have experienced unexplainable phenomena; God,
psychic abilities, extraordinary healing and angelic encounters.
Can cutting-edge science actually explain phenomena
previously thought of as 'paranormal'?
Paperback: 978-1-90504-793-2

The Vagabond Spirit of Poetry
Edward Clarke
Spend time with the wisest poets of the modern age and of the
past, and let Edward Clarke remind you of the importance of
poetry in our industrialized world.
Paperback: 978-1-78279-370-0 ebook: 978-1-78279-369-4

Readers of ebooks can buy or view any of these bestsellers by
clicking on the live link in the title. Most titles are published
in paperback and as an ebook. Paperbacks are available in
traditional bookshops. Both print and ebook formats are
available online. Find more titles and sign up to our readers'
newsletter at http://www.johnhuntpublishing.com/non-fiction
Follow us on Facebook at
https://www.facebook.com/JHPNonFiction
and Twitter at https://twitter.com/JHPNonFiction